The Confessions of

Three
Ebony
Bishops

The Confessions of

Three Ebony Bishops

EDSEL A. AMMONS
ERNEST S. LYGHT
JONATHAN D. KEATON

Abingdon Press
Nashville

THE CONFESSIONS OF THREE EBONY BISHOPS

Copyright © 2008 by Abingdon Press

This book is printed on acid-free paper.

Library of Congress Cataloging-in-Publication Data

Ammons, Edsel A.
    The confessions of three ebony bishops / Edsel A. Ammons, Ernest S. Lyght, Jonathan D. Keaton.
        p. cm.
    ISBN 978-0-687-64847-4 (pbk. : alk. paper)
    1. Christian leadership—United Methodist Church (U.S.) 2. Ammons, Edsel A. 3. Lyght, Ernest S., 1934– 4. Keaton, Jonathan D. I. Lyght, Ernest S., 1934– II. Keaton, Jonathan D. III. Title.
    BX8349.L43A46 2008
    262'.1276—dc22

2008000283

08 09 10 11 12 13 14 15 16 17—10 9 8 7 6 5 4 3 2 1
MANUFACTURED IN THE UNITED STATES OF AMERICA

CONTENTS

ACKNOWLEDGMENTS

To say that this book is about "three Ebony Bishops" overstates the case. Parents and siblings and significant others in our extended families, alive here or in the church triumphant, dwell in our words, phrases, stories, and testimonies. More than these, the book is about those whom we serve and lead. Most important, it is a response to God's call. None better do we know than the "God of our weary years." It is God whose power, grace, and forgiveness guide the work and witness of Bishops Edsel Albert Ammons, Ernest Shaw Lyght, and Jonathan Doyle Keaton.

Not subjoined to the list of authors is a gifted ebony colleague, Bishop Alfred Johnson. He made invaluable contributions to this work through critique and affirmation of its content, chapter format, personal encouragement, and prayer. We give thanks for him.

Also, Bishop Lyght deserves a special note of thanks. His passion, push, and determination to have us write a book resulted in additional tasks of coordination with us, the publisher, and the copy editor.

Particular thanks is due Executive Administrative Assistant, Mrs. Diane Allarding of the Michigan Area. From setting up conference calls and e-mailing texts to faxing and making phone calls, Diane made an invaluable contribution to the project.

Finally, we make this offering of gratitude to the whole church, especially the Black Church. In its music, worship, preaching, and advocacy, we were formed and shaped for service to the whole church. The book is a thanksgiving for the debt we owe to Christ but cannot pay; nevertheless we fully acknowledge Christ's gift in and through us all the more.

Edsel A. Ammons

Ernest S. Lyght

Jonathan D. Keaton

INTRODUCTION

A question across The United Methodist Church asks why the many years of activity in search of methods leading to the growth of membership have led, instead, to what may be considered disappointing results. One answer—perhaps the primary answer—might be that the focus of our efforts has been limited in large measure to certain planning and development techniques. By our dedication to techniques and to their prominence among us, we have become creatures of our intuition engaged, thereby, in the celebration of the "work of our own hands." However, we cannot attribute our inability to build constituency solely to a combination of planning miscalculations. Rather, we must push beyond to something much more fundamental, to something closer to the nature of the church itself.

This *something* that is more fundamental is, in fact, the measure of transcendence or "quality of soul." Moreover, it has long been identified with the "Prayer of Humble Access," when the prayer was known for its inclusion in the service of Holy Communion: *We do not come to . . . the Table trusting in our own righteousness but in Your great and multiple mercies.* It is this address to God, confessional in its expression, that has assured for it a place "high and lifted up." Its nature is of the nature of the church, and every word and activity of the church gives it breath and spirit, gives purpose and substance to every prayer, and gives aspiration to growth and renewed faithfulness within the church's life and witness. It is the emphasis on God before whom we humbly bow, rather than on growth—about which we experience great anxiety—which will sustain the church through seasons of uncertainty about itself, including the present one.

The significance of an approach to issues about the church's numerical vitality that is confessional in its expression cannot be overstated. This conclusion has been reached by three United Methodist bishops ("Ebony Bishops," a name used to reflect their African American heritage). We are compelled to make a strong statement that there is a need for a change to a different language, which speaks less of the church's dilemma and more about how the church's fortunes relate to a spirituality that is grounded in confession and self-denial. May the change begin with ourselves in a prayer offered up to Almighty God in these words: *If it be your will, O God, send us in search of a new theory of organizational* development that may bless us, but beyond all else, drive us to our knees in confession before You who alone can love us in sufficiency and save us and the church now and forevermore.

—Edsel A. Ammons

Section One

MY SPIRITUAL JOURNEY

My Faith Journey

Edsel A. Ammons

There is a story of a man who went to see the famous psychiatrist Carl Jung. The man suffered from depression and wanted help. Jung told him to cut back his fourteen-hour workday to eight, go directly home after work, and spend evenings in his study, quiet and all alone. So the man tried. He went to his study, shut the door, read the books of famous authors, and listened to the music of well-known composers. After some weeks of this, he returned to Jung complaining that he could see no improvement. On learning how the man had spent his time, Jung said, "But you didn't understand. I didn't want you to be with famous authors and composers. I wanted you to be all alone with yourself." The man looked terrified and explained, "I can't think of any worse company." Jung replied, "Yes, but this is the self you inflict on other people fourteen hours a day."

I confess to you that the same thought crossed my mind as I began to write. But this is my story and my faith journey, and I wish to share it with you. There was little reason for anyone to suspect that a shy child named after the president of an automobile company would be drawn to any kind of career in the public arena—surely not a career in a most public place like the church. From earliest memory, I was a private person who found comfort in doing what Jung recommended to the man struggling with his depression, in being all alone with myself. Conversation with me was an exercise in verbal brevity—an economy of speech tending toward silence at every opportunity.

An equally decisive factor in my development was the ethos of the home into which I was born. There were no preachers around to compete for our attention. From the beginning, I can recall the sights and sounds of jazz musicians, their shiny and interesting instruments, their different forms of speech, and their music. Our modest apartment was literally a way station for those immersed in a world devoted to the entertainment of others whose dialogue was saturated with words and phrases like "augmented," "diminished," "four beats to the bar," "play it simple," "syncopation needs better expression," "fade out," "fade in," and other colorful but less familiar speech. I knew what "dissonance" was almost before I could reach the keys on the piano. My mother and father were musicians—both pianists. She was trained. He was not, having taught himself to play by listening to piano rolls and placing his fingers into the depressed keys. Years later my father and brother would become famous, my father as creator of the boogie-woogie piano style and my brother as a celebrated tenor saxophonist. I was thrilled by the music and those who played it with such effortless skill in our living room. And I remain a jazz buff to this very day. It would have surprised no one had I chosen to devote my life to a career in popular music. There was never a time, however, when I felt strongly inclined to follow in the footsteps of my father or my mother.

The pull on my life in another direction was starting to lodge in my spirit. Indeed, before I could begin to rationalize it or give any logical answers to anybody's questions, including my own, I started to reveal to my family and a few friends my very early and unformed interests in the ministry of the church, specifically, the preaching ministry. Among the earliest influences was the family physician. He occasionally chatted with me about what career future I was considering. The church was not what the doctor wanted to hear as my answer. With no effort to conceal his disappointment, he grunted: "Why would you do a thing like that, forsaking both medicine and money?" I had no answer to his question because I really did not understand my feelings myself. What I felt and shared was as much a mystery to me as it was to my doctor and others. I could not have known then what I am utterly clear about today: that the Holy Spirit has its own way, works its own timetable, and was bearing witness even then to my spirit, long before I possessed the capacity for reasoned insight. Dag Hammarskjöld, former Secretary General of the United Nations, said it best: "I don't know Who—or what—put the question. . . . I don't even remember answering. But at some moment I did answer Yes to Someone . . . and from that hour, I was certain that . . . my life, in self-surrender, had a goal."

I did not know and could not have explained to anybody what was but a faint glimmer of awakening self-awareness. Even if I had known, talking about myself would have demanded more than my fragile ego could have abided. Again, my early confession of interest in a public-service career was nothing short of miraculous, for nothing frightened me more than public discourse. Grade school simply extended the period of personal trauma, and I sought refuge in studying, reading, and maintaining good grades. Although teachers and parents applauded my good efforts and impressive scholarship, they did not realize that a deep estrangement and distance from community were my daily companions.

I must also acknowledge my profound indebtedness to my family. Though preoccupied most of the time with trying to keep life and limb together through the dark days of the Depression, my family was warm and accepting. I sensed their affection for my brother and me and their delight as I made my way through those early years without causing them pain or embarrassment. My brother and I never had to wonder if we were cared about. It was the undramatic yet steady affection of my family—mother, father, even though he was divorced from my mother and not living in our home, grandparents, aunts, uncles, cousins—that was the unassuming but primary influence in my life. Early on, in fact, I began to reflect their warmth in my own tenuous relationships with the few close friends I did have. As I have tried to sort out and understand the influences that ignited in me expressions of those early instincts about ministry and bring to harvest the seeds planted by the Holy Spirit, I have identified the generous heart of my family. And I am convinced that their graciousness was due to the unquestioned importance of the church.

The greatest influence helping to shape my future, after my family, was the church and its importance in our lives. There was little talk about it and fewer arguments about matters of doctrine and belief. Christianity was not an issue for intellectual haggling in our home. No one questioned the faith that Grandfather shared with us in song and poetry. It was the power underneath the stubborn resolve of a Depression-smitten family. It was simply assumed that we would attend and participate in the life of a congregation nearest to where we lived. (We were urban nomads who changed addresses often in search of affordable rent.) Nor did we limit ourselves to a particular denomination. During the first decade of my life, we worshiped with Baptist, Congregational Community, and several Methodist groups, and had learned to appreciate all of them. Grandmother, who usually made the decision where we worshiped, had decreed that we would avoid places that were "noisy and too emotional." Authentic spontaneity in response to word and song was acceptable. But, "I want to worship," she would often say, "not sit through a spectacle!" Thus, the church was an early and familiar part of my upbringing.

These influences I clearly affirm. Still, however, I really can only speculate on my call to ordained ministry. There was no "Damascus Road" intervention. It was more like the "Emmaus Road" for me. Awareness came in the course of the journey; was gradual in its unfolding. The early and unexplained aspiration evolved in stages and in varying degrees of certainty. The earliest moment of decision about the preaching ministry came when a pastor and some other junior high school kids said to me, "You should think about becoming a preacher." Those critical words of invitation found their way into my heart. I never forgot them and struggled with their meaning in the years that followed. Was it God's unquestioned call to me? Or did it compel something in me because it was the first time anyone outside of my family cared enough to be interested in what I did with my life?

My response to what I experienced as calling was accompanied by bewilderment (there were no models to emulate) and serious doubts about my ability to commit to a way that seemed then, and even now, to demand more than I could bring to it. What could an impaired creature like me offer to the sacred work of the ordained preacher of the gospel? The words of Saint Paul became my words to myself; I am the least of these called to be a preacher (1 Cor 15:9). For was I not, as already admitted, possessed of fragile ego and faltering speech? It occurred to me, of course, that Moses stuttered, but that was not my problem. Speech itself was my problem! Fashioning sentences and paragraphs was my torment resulting from an abysmal lack of self-confidence, a literal verbal paralysis that I would finally overcome late in my college years. "Of all people, why someone so unable as I?" was a familiar prayerful response to myself (having interesting biblical parallels). I have thought many times about that question. Each time I am reminded of God's use of ordinary, impaired people as instruments of gracious ministry. Indeed, "transformed ordinariness" is a legitimate definition of every priest, pastor, apostle of Christ. It was certainly true of me.

The late Thomas Merton, well-known Trappist monk, priest, poet, novelist, mystic, theologian, who probed the depths of spiritual understanding, had an interesting view of things we often label ordinary: "The real world, the one so obvious, that we no longer see it, so ordinary that we have not even looked at it for many years, is not only beautiful but romantically beautiful. It is romantic in the ordinariness, the banality that we ourselves tend to reject." In writing about spirituality in his essay titled "The Cell," Merton states that "one of the most important elements in the beginning of a spiritual life, the route of the contemplative, is the ability to see value and beauty in ordinary things, where the disciple reaches the point in which an illusion is stripped away and he knows his own weakness and the way is made clear for 'the moment of truth' in which a new identity is discovered in God." Merton saw all of life with an eye of faith.

My growth in spiritual maturity and discernment came grudgingly. My early enthusiasm began to wane, and, like Jacob, I began to wrestle with the angel that had watched over me. And what a wrestling match it was as I made my way through high school. They were generally happy years, but they became increasingly burdened with the beginning of a protracted period of doubt about the faith that had fed the early hungers of heart and head. A zealous acceptance of the faith once delivered by family and church collided with my determined will to know more about the world and myself and to have reasoned (meaning provable) answers to every question. There was a severe break with the fundamentalism of preachers and parents. And it should surprise no one that I threw out the baby with the bathwater.

It was a time of desert wandering happening at a point of passage from an age of innocence about myself and the world. I was becoming painfully aware of the high cost of being black and was struggling with the meaning of that for me personally and with my place in a world where there seemed to be little place for people of color—especially my color. It was a dilemma for which no teenager is prepared, and a terrible strain on a faith that had been steeped in an otherworldly optimism. I vividly remember the question that dogged me: Is it possible to be both black and Christian? It was an especially compelling time in my journey. I knew, with incredible clarity, what Saint Paul must have meant when he cried out in his own despair, "Wretched man that I am! Who will rescue me from this body of death?" (Rom 7:24). Wretchedness is the only way I can describe the suffering that comes when innocence confronts the evil of racism. The words of an old African American song were a constant companion: "I cried all night long, cried, until I found the Lord."

My parents never wavered in their acceptance of what they saw as the growing pains of an adolescent struggling to be an adult. Religious understanding remained in a state of arrested development though still a bedrock motivation to prayers routinely spoken at morning and evening hours. My high school speech teacher became the bridge over troubled waters. It was he who helped me take the first tenuous steps toward a more positive and hopeful self-image and a strong disavowal of the stigma of birth, which is the burden of every black child. "You're going places," he said to me one day following my first effort at making a speech in front of the class. From that moment, I began to dream of almost forbidden possibilities that I had never before imagined.

As often happens, inspiration evoked aspiration. High school concluded on a high note. But college was another story. In fact, World War II had become a daily diversion. The unsettling approach of the draft left little energy for scholarship. Soon I became a young adult in a military uniform with a dream and an embattled faith in God. What would happen to the dream—and the dreamer?

It was that same faith—tested in many ways—that sustained soul and body through three years of military service. Return to civilian life was aligned with disappointment over time lost and suspicion that God really did intend a very different future for me than the one I had imagined as a child. But the hunger could not be assuaged. The call would not be silenced, and I pressed on toward the "calling of the High Call." With my civilian life in somewhat manageable order, I completed college and the first two years of seminary study, yet still questioning. Then, short of money and married, I left seminary and left behind forever, I thought, any chance of a significant career as a preacher of the gospel.

I did accept appointment to a small (thirty-eight-member) African American Methodist congregation. It was, in fact, a weekend preaching responsibility with people I had known since Sunday school years. A place to preach while I held full-time jobs is what it really was. But, as disappointing as that seemed to me, it served to keep alive the hope in me of better days ahead and that God's purpose for me was still unfolding. My suspicion seemed all the more confirmed in subsequent events that would change the fabric and direction of my life.

From that time to this moment, I have not looked back nor have I ever doubted that I am being sent and led by the Holy Spirit into the work of ministry for which God created me. A very ordinary and self-deprecating instrument, transformed by the mercy of God in whom I have learned to trust and, trusting, have been able to feel certain of my calling and my capacity to live out that calling through the church as a leader of congregations or in whatever forms my ministry would take.

My life within a denominational system has taken several directions. Both of my ordinations (deacon and elder) have happened in an African

Methodist setting at the hands of a black bishop who would serve as a model for my own episcopacy later in my life. Following a year in an appointment to a small congregation, I returned home to complete the final year of seminary education and to seek employment to supplement a meager income. My job and a full schedule of classes at the seminary left little time for academic endeavor of any kind or for worry about my pastoral future. I decided to focus on completing the courses that graduation required and to address the other issues as I was able.

During the early morning hours of one of those short nights, another event in my faith journey happened that determined the final course and direction of the journey. It was a phone call from a district superintendent of the Rock River Annual Conference of the Methodist Church. A small congregation in his district was living through racial change in the community, and the congregation was reflecting the effects of the change in its own life. I had been recommended as someone who might help the congregation live responsibly through the uncertainties that were just ahead. Would I consider it? It was one of the easiest decisions I would ever have to make. I said yes before hearing any of the details! It proved to be one of the wisest decisions of my life. The consequences have been many and far-reaching, taking me through virtually every phase of the life of a global church, comprising fifty years of "labor of love" and a life of grace and joy in the service of our blessed Lord, Jesus Christ.

My Spiritual Journey

Ernest S. Lyght

God bless my parents! The loving presence and spiritual influence of my mother and father helped shape me into who I am today. Their parental influence has continued to shape me over the years, and that influence is ever present. I learned from them. I was encouraged and supported by them in all of my endeavors during their lifetimes. I suspect that their influence has been manifested in my two children, although they only enjoyed a few brief years together. I am indebted to my parents, and I am grateful for all of their gifts bequeathed to me and my three siblings.

The Context

My spiritual journey is a three-generational spiritual autobiography whose inception is rooted in the rich heritage of Methodism as manifested on Maryland's Eastern Shore. John Wesley's Methodism readily took root in the fertile spiritual climate among black and white people there, who worked either as farmers or watermen or in some related industry. The circuit-riding preachers were ever present, and congregations cropped up in almost every village and town. In many instances, there would be at least two Methodist churches in a particular locale, one black and one white. The congregational settings mirrored the segregated structures of the U.S. American society of that time.

The camp meeting was also a part of the Methodist experience on the Eastern Shore. The camp meeting phenomenon, as a spiritual oasis, lasted well into the 1960s and influenced the lives of Methodists and non-Methodists alike, black and white. It influenced my life as well.

After the 1939 uniting conference, merging the Methodist Church North, the Methodist Church South, and the Methodist Protestant Church, the black Methodist congregations on Maryland's Eastern Shore remained in the Delaware Conference. This conference was made a part of the new Central Jurisdiction, which was defined by race. The neighboring white Methodist congregations remained in the Peninsula Conference, which was made a part of the Northeastern Jurisdiction that was defined by geography.

The walls of segregation were real in the Methodist church and in the society and culture of America well into the sixth decade of the twentieth century. The realities of segregation had an impact on my parents, but they did not succumb to its harsh pressures. They did not become bitter, nor did they teach their children to hate white people. Instead, we were taught to love our neighbors and to accept all people.

Family Roots

My parents, William and Attrue Lyght, were reared and educated in this milieu. They first met when they were students at the Princess Anne Academy (now the University of Maryland Eastern Shore), a secondary school founded by the Delaware Conference in the rural community of Princess Anne, Maryland. During their years in school, the Academy was headed by Reverend Kiah, a Methodist minister. Under his leadership, the school provided a profound spiritual influence on its students through its clear sense of purpose. This sense of purpose was manifested through the teaching and example of a dedicated faculty and staff.

Both of my parents grew up in Methodist families and attended the local Methodist church near their respective homes. Attrue grew up at Waters Chapel near Kingston, Maryland. The church was located directly across the road from her home. Both of her parents were members of the Waters Chapel Methodist Episcopal Church as well, and it was part of the family ritual to attend worship on a weekly basis.

William grew up in a rural area outside of Cambridge, Maryland. He called it "The Big Woods." The small village near the family homestead was called The Mission, and the Methodist church was located there. My father's formal education began at The Mission's Methodist church, where his mother was his first classroom teacher. Church was always a part of his life and experience.

After graduating from the high school at Princess Anne Academy, Attrue completed two years of college at the Academy. When she left the Academy, she went to Orange, New Jersey, where she stayed for several years doing domestic work with various white families. She found time in the midst of this experience to complete a course in secretarial work, gaining proficiency in typing and shorthand. When William completed high school at the Academy, he went on to Morgan College, now Morgan State University, a Methodist college in Baltimore. William, who had dropped out of high school to help support his family, graduated from high school at age twenty-six. This was a significant time in his life since he answered God's call to ordained ministry, completed his bachelor's degree at Morgan College, and graduated from Drew Theological Seminary in Madison, New Jersey, in 1933 with a master of divinity degree.

When my parents married on October 10, 1934, they brought together a common heritage of rural life and the Methodist church and its camp meeting tradition. Interestingly, both of my parents were reared in single-parent homes. My father was raised by his mother and older siblings, while my mother was reared by her father and paternal aunt. This experience fostered in both a deep devotion to family as they reared their own children. My father became the consummate breadwinner, whereas my mother chose to be a homemaker. In parenting, though, they were partners.

The Early Years

I was born into a Christian family on September 15, 1943. Since my father was an itinerant Methodist minister, I was reared in four different parsonages located in different cities and states (Princess Anne, Maryland; Chester, Pennsylvania; Atlantic City, New Jersey; and Wilmington, Delaware). I was the youngest of my parents' children.

The philosopher Will James would have called me a "once-born Christian." Even before I was baptized as an infant, my parents took me to church at Metropolitan Methodist Church in Princess Anne, Maryland. Over time I learned how to behave in church by going to church and observing older children and adults and by adhering to family discipline. I also was learning about "church" through personal participation in the life of the congregation.

As I grew, various adults in the church family manifested a genuine interest in me as a young person. Sunday school was a very positive experience in my life. I remain grateful to my Sunday school teachers who poured their time, energy, and spirit into their teaching and students. One person in particular, the Sunday school superintendent at Asbury Methodist Church, Atlantic City, was a saint. Vacation Bible school each year provided two enjoyable weeks of wholesome fun, learning, and growing.

I enjoyed going to church because it was a safe place to go, and the people were so friendly. It was a place where people demonstrated their care about children and youth through their actions and words. For example, at Asbury Church, even as a child I was invited to the communion rail on Communion Sunday. It was an awesome experience. It was a spiritual experience, but I did not know that then. I know now that the adults were showing the children that they were welcome in all aspects of the church.

Communion Sunday was a very special time, and the attendance would swell on each first Sunday. The chancel area was covered with white apparel, and the communion stewardesses were dressed in freshly starched white dresses or uniforms. Communion Sunday was a holy time that required your presence, your participation, and your intention to lead a new life following God's commandments as you walked with Jesus. I did not understand the ultimate meaning of Holy Communion as a child. Through the years, I have gained a much deeper understanding of this sacrament. I continue to grow in my understanding, always realizing that it is, indeed, a "holy mystery." This is a matter of God's amazing grace.

As a child, I learned how the music of worship communicates God's love and care. Like many people, I learned the words to many hymns simply because we frequently sang them during the Sunday worship. Moreover, people quoted from hymns in their personal testimonies and prayers, sometimes even lining several verses. The preacher often quoted a hymn as a means of illustrating a sermonic point. One hymn in particular has stayed with me since childhood, "Come Ye Disconsolate," which my father, who was also my pastor, often used as an invitational hymn. Each time I heard this song, I was convinced God could heal all things. Now I know from personal experience that God is a healing God and is always with us. Numerous worship services began with the congregation singing "Holy, Holy, Holy." I could feel the very presence of God in the majesty of the moment and the sacredness of the worship space. We were in the presence of God, and we were standing on holy ground.

I learned to pray at church while listening to the prayers of the preacher and the prayers of the people. My parents, of course, taught me to pray at home by reciting the Lord's Prayer. They also taught me to pray brief prayers of thanksgiving, regarding the good things that happened in my small world as a child. Prayer was a part of the ritual of preparation prior to every meal in our home. We were urged daily to give thanks for all of God's goodness and bounty. Usually, my father would offer the prayer before our Sunday dinner. Typically, this was an extended prayer of thanksgiving and praise, followed by a prayer that blessed the meal and gave thanks for God's bountiful goodness.

The pastoral prayers that I heard at church ushered me into a larger world. Many of those pastoral prayers came from my father's lips. I came to understand that there were people around me, as well as people at a distance, who were hurting and suffering. I learned that prayer is a sincere and frank conversation with God. Without a doubt, my posture toward prayer was formulated as a child and nurtured during my teenage years. I am still learning the meaning of prayer and seeking to further develop a disciplined prayer life. I have come to appreciate deeply the notion and practice of "having a little talk with Jesus."

As a youth, I joined Asbury Methodist Church in Atlantic City, New Jersey. There was no confirmation class. The pastor, however, mentored the children and prepared them to join the church. At the time, I attended worship and Sunday school each Sunday, sang in the children's choir, and participated in other church activities for youth. We went to church at least twice on Sunday. Those were formative years from 1951 to 1954.

My father became a district superintendent in 1955 when I was in sixth grade. We moved to Wilmington, Delaware, where my sister and I attended Haven Methodist Church with our mother. During that six-year tenure of Dad's superintendency we had two pastors, the Reverends M. L. McKinney and H. T. Moody. Among other things, both pastors were strongly supportive of the youth. We knew that they cared about young people and wanted us to be a part of the church in a meaningful way.

Teenagers at Haven Methodist Church were invited to participate in the Sunday service as readers on a fairly regular basis. As a result, we learned to comfortably read and speak in public. From the encouragement we received, we gained self-confidence and grew physically and spiritually. I also participated in weekly youth fellowship and district youth meetings that occurred during the year. Each summer, I attended a conference youth rally where I met people from around the Delaware Conference, which included parts of Pennsylvania, New York, New Jersey, and Maryland, as well as the whole state of Delaware. We learned about the Bible and how to apply the Scripture lessons to our teenage experiences of daily living. These experiences were the beginning of my leadership training.

The summer months ushered in the camp meeting season on the Eastern Shore of Maryland. As children, we enjoyed going to the camp meetings because we anticipated seeing our maternal grandfather, Dad Lo (Logan). My grandfather, who drove a school bus during the school year, used his bus to transport camp meeting participants during the summer season. There was a camp meeting in a black Methodist church every Sunday, from the beginning of June through the end of September. When we hit the campground, we would go in search of his bus and the picnic baskets of food that everyone had on board. After we had eaten some good food, Dad Lo would take us to get a treat, an ice cream cone or a soda. For us it was like a family reunion.

My father was a frequent preacher at the various camp meetings, usually at the afternoon tent meeting service. I used to stand on the sideline and watch the happenings. Between worship services, the praying/singing bands would gather on the campground somewhere near the church building or the outdoor meeting tent. My aunt, Dad's sister, sang with one of the bands. Dressed in her white apron, she would join in the long choruses and the fervent prayers. These praying/singing experiences sometimes lasted for several hours and often into the night. Even as a young child, I could see that not everyone who entered the camp meeting grounds came there for spiritual reasons. Whereas some people came to worship God, some came to carouse with the devil. I came to know the difference by observation. Some people even adroitly fluctuated between the two poles, but that was a manifestation of life's struggle and the church's effort to "beat the devil."

The High School Years

During high school, I began exploring the possibility of ministry as a calling. Pastoral ministry as a vocation had always been visible to me since my father was a pastor. Individual laypeople and some ministers began to raise the question of ministry with me. At the time, I had no idea that I would later accept God's call and enter ordained ministry. Nevertheless, I would go to the altar during the annual ordination service at annual conference along with other young people who were exploring the ordained ministry as a call. While in high school I was licensed as a local preacher, and would occasionally accept an invitation to serve as the preacher for a youth day at a Methodist church. I was growing in the faith and thinking more seriously about the future and what it might hold for me.

My years at Wilmington High School in Wilmington, Delaware, were filled with activity and fun. I enjoyed high school. I was on the college-prep track, and participated in several sports as well. I was a member of the basketball, football, and track teams. Track, though, was my best sport, and I even managed to win a state championship in junior high and again in high school. Participation in sports helped me learn personal discipline, team participation, achievement (that is, winning and losing), and leadership. In addition, I was an active participant in my high school student government through the student council. This experience provided additional lessons in participation and cooperation as well as opportunities for leadership.

My introduction to playing a musical instrument did not go well. My father tried teaching me to play the piano, but I was a reluctant student. However, I did learn to play the tuba and participated in the band and orchestra. Music helped broaden my perspective about life. I have learned that life is, indeed, a kind of symphony that is based on relationships, cooperation, and participation.

Although I attended a public high school, I became a kind of unofficial chaplain in my all-boys homeroom class. Our teacher was a deacon in his church, and each day we read Scripture and said the Lord's Prayer, along with our salute to the American flag. This was prior to the Supreme Court decision banning prayer in public schools. Although I frequently read Scripture, I did not realize this experience was preparing me for ministry.

Bound for College

It was a given in our household that the four Lyght children would go to college. My high school years, therefore, were focused on preparation for college. In my senior year, I applied to Morgan State College in Baltimore and was accepted for the fall of 1961. When I arrived on campus, my sister Celestine, a sophomore, helped me make a positive adjustment to campus life.

Like most college freshmen, I was delighted to be away from home and experiencing a freedom that I had never known before. I alternated church attendance between the Morgan Christian Center, which was on campus, and the Northwood Methodist Church, located a few blocks from the campus. At the beginning of my second year, I decided that I would focus my church participation at the Christian Center, where the Reverend Howard Cornish, a Methodist minister, was the chaplain.

Reverend Cornish made me his unofficial assistant because he knew that I was exploring the possibility of ministry. On most Sundays I served as the liturgist, which helped me gain confidence as a worship leader. As I was learning to read the Scriptures aloud publicly and to lead prayers in worship, I continued growing in Christ.

Participation at worship in the Christian Center exposed me to a number of dynamic preachers and scholars who visited our campus. Among these luminaries were Howard Thurman, Mordecai Johnson, Henry Crane, Will Herberg, William Sloane Coffin, and George Outen. These preachers challenged my faith and helped me better understand what it meant to be a disciple of Jesus Christ.

During college, I served as president of the Schweitzer Club for preministerial students, and the Wesley Club, one of several student religious groups on campus. Participating in these groups provided nurturing experiences along my spiritual journey and more opportunities to learn about leadership. My experience with mandatory Army ROTC also helped me develop as a leader. Although I was glad to leave ROTC, I left with a better understanding of basic leadership dynamics.

College in the 1960s was a volatile yet memorable time. It was during the height of the civil rights movement when I arrived in Baltimore in September 1961. Black people arriving by train had to go to the end of the taxi line and wait until all white patrons had been served. The shopping mall across the street from Morgan State was open to all shoppers, except for the theater, which was segregated. During my sophomore year, the students decided to picket the Northwood Theater. As a result, several hundred students were arrested and incarcerated in the Baltimore city jail in lieu of bail. I was one of the students arrested on that Monday evening. After our release the following Thursday and after subsequent, long negotiations, the theater management capitulated to our demands and integrated. Several months passed, though, before I patronized the theater again.

The call to ministry was becoming more dynamic and magnetic. By my senior year, it was clear that God was calling me to ordained ministry. I decided that it was time to apply to theological school, so I applied and was accepted to Drew University.

Seminary and Ordination

The call to ministry for me was a slow evolution. There was no dramatic moment, only the slow unfolding drama of answering God's call. There was no Damascus Road experience. There was, however, the quiet voice of God beckoning me to enter the ministry. There were, of course, various saints along the way who helped me hear God's call. They encouraged and nudged me in the right direction. Reverend Cornish, the college chaplain, was one of those people. Another person was Dr. Richard I. McKinney, my philosophy professor and an ordained Baptist minister, who encouraged me to strive for excellence. He also encouraged a deeply rooted spiritual foundation in me.

My parents quietly supported me in my academic pursuits and my spiritual development. On the one hand, I can see that my mother in her quiet way was in a real sense the fiber of my spirituality. On the other hand, my father was the manifestation of what it meant to be a spiritual leader. Dad was the preacher, but Mom was the quiet presence.

At Drew, I met many new friends from across the nation. The academic experience was rigorous and rewarding. I learned to think with more discipline and exploration and had the opportunity to experience a variety of theological viewpoints. My roots in the African American tradition of Christianity and culture helped me keep my mind staid on Jesus. Faith for me was a matter of the Father, the Son, and the Holy Spirit. These three were and continue to be the anchors of my credo. A comprehensive theological education assisted me in my journey to the cross to meet Jesus in a new and fresh way.

By my graduation from Drew in May 1968, the majority of the theological school faculty had tendered their resignations. The faculty exodus was the culmination of a bitter struggle between the administration and the seminary dean and his faculty. I, along with other seminarians, participated in numerous meetings and demonstrations, imploring the administration to resolve the conflict. We wanted the administration and the board of trustees to be fair and just with the theological school in matters of budget and endowment.

The faculty exodus disrupted my plans to remain at Drew in the doctoral program. Since the professors whom I wanted to study with had left, so did I and, instead, entered a master's program at Princeton Seminary. That decision turned my course in a different direction. In many ways it was the reason I remained in pastoral ministry and did not follow a teaching career.

In my middle year at Drew, my application for ordination as a deacon was accepted. The Peninsula Conference ordained me as a deacon in 1966 and as an elder in 1968. My ordaining bishop was Bishop John Wesley Lord. When he ordained me as an elder, he invited my father to join him in the laying on of hands. At that session of the annual conference, Dad retired as a conference member, and I was received into conference membership. In a real sense, he passed the mantle of full-time ministry to me. That was a spiritual moment that I will cherish always.

An Abiding Parental Influence

My mother and father were spiritual giants in my life. Mom was a quiet and gentle spirit. She was always present because she was a full-time homemaker. Her love was patient and kind. She spent a lot of time with me going over my spelling lessons. Dad was the breadwinner and the disciplinarian. He was gone a lot, especially when he was a district superintendent. If he was not home at our bedtime, we knew that he would come to our room before going to bed himself. We could count on that. Interestingly, although Mom had very gentle hands, we did not go to her to tend to our cuts and scratches; Dad was the family first-aid person. My father was the spiritual leader at home as well as in the church and community. He practiced a tough love, but he was kind and always the encourager. Many times I saw him go out of his way to help people who needed a helping hand.

Both of my parents had a specific prayer time and meditation period. Sunday dinner was the time when Dad would offer an extended family prayer, followed by the family reciting the Lord's Prayer. Then there would be the blessing of the food. My parents' spirituality was ever present and influenced my growth and development. They are a part of who I am today. I am grateful for the experience of being nurtured by two loving parents, whose spirituality continues to illumine my spiritual path.

The Continuing Journey

The spiritual journey for me is a continuing process that has been nurtured by various partners along the way. During my first pastoral appointment, I attended the Wednesday night union prayer service, which was an African American ecumenical service. This was an inspiring experience for a young pastor, because I was exposed to some of the living saints from the various participating congregations. Their witness helped me gain a deeper understanding of how some Christians are able to face the difficulties of life they encounter. As I listened to their prayers, I learned more about how to engage in conversation with God. These folk were my partners on the spiritual path with Jesus.

During my third pastoral appointment, I led a weekly Bible study group that met in the homes of various members. The group consisted of a retired minister, young people, middle-aged adults, and older adults. These individuals were seeking to learn more about the Bible as they sought to be faithful disciples in a complex world. They helped me delve more deeply into the meaning of the biblical texts as we explored various books of the Bible. They were my discipleship partners long before I encountered DISCIPLE *Bible Study*.

The ten years that I served as pastor at St. Mark's United Methodist Church (1979–1989) were formative years for me. I was able to take a fresh look at my weaknesses and forge some of them into strengths. The congregation played a crucial role in this process, especially the Tuesday evening prayer group. I seldom missed one of their meetings or Bible study sessions. It was always an inspirational experience where I encountered people who were living their lives as a conversation with God. Their prayers helped strengthen me on the spiritual journey. We were prayer partners and partners in ministry.

While the resident bishop in the New York Area, I was privileged to participate in DISCIPLE I with the extended Cabinet. This yearlong exploration opened our hearts and minds to new vistas of understanding regarding discipleship, mission, and the spiritual life. We grew in our understanding of the Bible, nurturing one another and being nurtured by the Holy Spirit. We grew in our Christian fellowship. We became partners in a joint learning experience.

Jonathan Keaton and I are members of the class of bishops elected in 1996. Almost from the beginning of our tenure in the Council of Bishops

(COB), we made a covenant to walk together each morning when we attend a COB meeting or other meetings together. Quite often, other colleagues will join us on these walks. We participate in fellowship together. We meditate together. We pray together, and we have become spiritual partners. We have been inspired by the prayers of Bishop Edsel Ammons, whom we adopted as our spiritual partner and mentor. These colleagues, along with others, have helped me stay on the spiritual path with Jesus.

Leadership

As a child, I did not envision myself as a leader, nor did I see myself as a leader during my college and seminary years. Nevertheless, my capacity for leadership was being nurtured through my varied experiences. I can remember how I admired many of the clergy leaders of the annual conference in Southern New Jersey and, later, in the Northern New Jersey Conference. Then one day I realized that I was among the clergy leaders of the annual conference. This leadership was manifested in my spiritual leadership as a local church pastor, a district superintendent, and a general superintendent.

MY SPIRITUAL JOURNEY

Jonathan D. Keaton

As Timothy (2 Tim 1:5) came to faith under the influence of his grandmother Lois and mother, Eunice, my religious perspective developed under the guidance of my grandmother Martha T. Harris-Reed and mother, Euba M. Harris-Winton. Mother and Mama (my grandmother) were stalwart Methodists, children of the Black Church and servant leaders before, during, and after the dawn of the Central Jurisdiction in 1939. Together and separately, they made decisions that shaped the faith journey of my siblings and me. They often spoke about the reality of God. As God cared about the world, so He cared about us. God's Son could be depended upon to feed, care for, and protect us. And if we believed in Jesus the Christ strongly enough and did what was right, any obstacle we faced due to the color of our skin could be overcome. My grandmother had the greatest influence in creating a religious environment in our house, instilling a strong work ethic in me, and focusing me on my *call* to ministry. My mother's impact on my life was different but just as significant in several areas. She sent us to Catholic school, shared her love of music with us, and as a Black Community Developer with the General Board of Global Ministries (GBGM), provided an outstanding example of servant leadership in the *practice* of ministry. My grandmother and my mother were equally passionate about getting a good education and serving the Black Church.

When I left home for good, the foundation laid by my mother and grandmother was changed and transformed, primarily throughout my experiences at Philander Smith College and Garrett-Evangelical Seminary, and the ordination process of the Northern Illinois Conference. Each experience functioned as a crucible to hammer out and further refine my belief in God, the church, the world, myself, and my status as an African American.

Mama (Our Name for Grandmother)

My grandmother exerted great influence over my life. Mother was single with a growing family; money was scarce, and so to survive we lived with Mama. Often, Mother worked two or three jobs "to make ends meet." Since work took Mother away from home, Mama assumed major responsibility for raising most of her daughter's ten children. Mama worked too. She did "day work" for white families who employed her to clean their houses, cook their food, and help raise their children. Although friends helped Mother and Mama with childcare when both of them were working, Mama was the parental force to be reckoned with. Her approach to parenting evolved in three movements: love, rules, and church.

First, she helped Mother with childcare. Raising two to three young babies simultaneously required love, sacrifice, and commitment. Mama bonded with her grandchildren and loved us unconditionally.

Second, my grandmother established a set of rules to live by, and she held every child accountable for them. Chores were performed daily. Saturday was the primary cleaning day. If responsibility was shirked, then the culprit paid the price. Although playing dominoes and card games of every sort was strictly forbidden, we often sneaked and played cards. One day Mama came home to discover us playing a card game known as Old Maid. She turned over the card table declaring that we were gambling and that gambling was not allowed in her house. We never understood that rationale, but were forced to follow her rules.

Mother and Mama expected us to speak kindly and correctly to one another. Bad language and cursing found no place at that house in Fort Smith, Arkansas (even if we were mad). All our meals had to be eaten together, at the table. We prayed, ate, and talked together. At any given time, six to seven kids sat at the table along with Mother and Mama. An often-repeated phrase that Mother and Mama lived by was "a family that prays together, stays together."

Third, church played a dominant role in both Mother's and Mama's lives, and as a result, it played a major role in our lives as well. They made a commitment to have us in church every time the doors opened. My mother asserted, "We don't have a lot of money, but you can serve." Mama, whose late husband served as pastor of Mallalieu United Methodist Church, also believed in serving her church. By the time her grandchildren arrived, Mama was a communion steward. Every first Sunday, the stewards washed and filled the communion goblets, set the wafers in place, and dressed the altar in white. Then they donned their starched, white, and immaculately pressed communion dresses and assisted the pastor during communion. More than once, I heard my grandmother celebrate the fact that God had allowed her to make "one more communion." Sundays were little Easters in our house. Everybody got up, dressed, and went to church. Each of us served and participated in some capacity. After church, we walked home looking forward to dinner as a family. Every Sunday Mama made homemade rolls. What we lacked in a well-rounded diet, we found in the delightful taste of those hot rolls smothered in butter and jelly. For many reasons in my house, Sunday was a joy.

My youthful innocence about church and serving the church changed when Mama began announcing to her friends that I was going to be a preacher. For me, this sudden announcement had no context or rationale. I never dared ask my grandmother why she did this. All I knew was a burden had been laid on me without consultation. Her declaration, though, made me aware that I had a decision to make. I could accept or reject her pronouncement. I chose the latter. Afterward, the bond between us grew stronger on most things, but around the area of vocational choice, our relationship was strained for many years.

While I protested Mama's conviction that I would be a preacher like my grandfather, she continued unheeded to promote this vision to others. As a result of her promptings and my protests, inner conversations with an unseen God began dogging my conscience and consciousness. I heard a distinct call to ministry. I refused, however, to acknowledge this to my grandmother. Until I yielded to God's call a year after Mama died, I could not even admit it to myself. Until I penned these reflections, I had not even realized that Mama had stopped bugging me about the ministry during my college years. Instead she went underground, satisfied that she had planted in my heart and mind the call to ministry. Simply put, the only question that remained concerned the sprouting of that seed. A year after Mama's death, the seed sprouted, and I said yes to God's call.

Most of what I learned about God and God's ways from Mama reached its apex during my first year at Philander Smith College. For the first time in my life, I lived in a place other than my grandmother's house. Being apart from her was traumatic. In addition, I knew her health was failing.

25

So we kept in touch through letters. I still have eight of her handwritten letters, which are dated from September 21, 1966, to May 3, 1967—twenty-three days before her death. Here are a few of her last lessons.

> *October 2, 1966:* I am glad the Lord spared me to see you enter college. I hope you will have the spirit to make it through. I am praying for you. I have the faith to believe that it will. Now I am hoping and praying for your success and I believe our prayers will be heard. So keep on going to church and trusting the Lord always and continue to do the right thing. May the Lord bless you and keep you safe. With lots of Love, From Mama, Your grandmother.

Mama talked about faith, the church, prayer, success, and doing the right thing. By intent, she chose not to mention my being a preacher. Also, I was struck by her gratitude to God for my entering Philander Smith College, a black college supported by the Methodist Church. In fact, I had stayed home with Mama and attended Fort Smith Junior College for two years prior to my attending Philander. Mama hung her hopes on Philander—that it would push me toward the call. She was right.

> *October 23, 1966:* I am thrilled with the work you are doing. [In the Work/Study program—I got a job in the Religious Life Office at Philander Smith College.] I am hoping and praying for a wonderful success for you. If you mean good and I believe you do, I don't see how you can miss. . . . Always hoping and praying for the best for you. In Jesus' name, Mama your grandmother.

Mama mentioned hope, faith, success, belief in me, and the name of Jesus. Again, she wrote nothing about my entering the ministry.

> *January 18, 1967:* I am glad the sum I sent you helped you when you needed it most; I wish I could do more. I am not like some looking for it back in dollars and cents but I am looking for it in your success and the good that you may do to help uplift others. I have faith to believe it will [be] that way. . . . May the Lord bless you and keep you inspired— lovingly Mama

Mama had made sure that my notions of success were not connected to self-aggrandizement. Whatever so-called success I might attain ought to be used to uplift others. Seven major themes ran through all her letters: faith, hope, love, success, prayer, work, and serving or helping others.

Mama believed in God. She believed that God cared about the world and me as an individual and that God would watch over and protect me. Though she never mentioned the ministry in her last letters, the seed had been planted. Initially, I thought Mama bugged me about the ministry for her own personal reasons, namely, so I would follow in my grandfather's footsteps. However, thirty-nine years of reflection have led me to a different conclusion. Mama called me into ministry because God made her an instrument for calling one of her grandsons into the ministry of Jesus Christ. Literally and figuratively, she could do no other. With Mother, though, it was a different story.

Mother

While the circumstances of my mother's life offered the opportunity for my grandmother to exert great influence over my life, there were limits. Mama focused on specific areas of life and well-being. Mother functioned in a similar way. However, I find it difficult to identify specific places where Mother had an impact on my life. For all her dynamism, she rarely shared her innermost thoughts with me or my siblings. More often than not, she believed that we knew what she thought, but we didn't. Moreover, I rarely asked, particularly during the first forty years of my life. Things, though, have changed in the last nineteen years. I have learned more about her thoughts, but only since I have risked asking about them.

Many of my learnings about Mother are the result of an event, experience, or emotional memory. For example, when I was fifty-nine, I learned that when I was born, she placed me on her stomach and gave me back to God. Such key reflections about my spiritual journey have only recently come to light.

In 1961, Mother married for a third time and moved with my brothers and sisters to a new home. She offered me the choice of staying with Mama or moving with her. For me it was an easy choice: I stayed with Mama. Just as Mother refrained from choosing a vocation for me, she allowed me the freedom of this choice as well. For me, this freedom was an act of grace. I finished high school and, in 1964, attended Fort Smith Junior College for two years, and then entered Philander Smith College in the fall of 1966. Nine months later, Mama died. The pain I felt then and now, God has addressed over time. At the time, no one told me that Mama had been rushed to the hospital with a stroke or that she was dying. My only chance to utter the final words I would have spoken to Mama had been said during my frequent trips to her grave. My mother asked Beverly, my girlfriend and the woman I would marry in 1969, to break the news to me about Mama. It was during final exams, and no one wanted to disturb me with such heartbreaking news. But I was disturbed nevertheless. From the day I learned of Mama's death until the day I accepted God's call to ministry, the inner struggle to reject ministry and embrace medicine increased tenfold. The turmoil almost tore me apart and only abated when I relented. The title of a play being performed on Broadway at the time sums up my struggle: *Your Arms Too Short to Box with God.*

Serving Christ and His Church

When it came to the practice of ministry, Mother got involved in people's lives. Her mission was and is "to help people who fall through the cracks." Her social concerns included a range of areas including racism, gang violence, hunger, housing, job discrimination, education reform, immigrant rights, drug abuse, AIDS, voter registration, discrimination against women and children, and so on. Using her knowledge and passion for the downtrodden, Mother became an articulate spokesperson for people needing a voice. She spoke to and with power. If church, civic, government, judicial, or black leaders created obstacles for the helpless, she confronted them. If Mother needed to use her elected office to further the cause, she did so. Down through the years, I have heard many reports of her passionate witness on the Commission on Religion and Race, the Commission on the Status and Role of Women, the North Arkansas United Methodist Women (president), the Fort Smith chapter of the NAACP (vice-chair), and Justice of the Peace. She was named one of ten Matriarchs of the state of Arkansas in 1989 because her ministry touched an ever widening community of persons without regard to race, creed, color, gender, nationality, sexual orientation, or circumstance. Yet, no title gave Mother greater satisfaction than the one that launched her into public ministry in 1970. She became a Black Community Developer with the General Board of Global Ministries. Mother's life skills and experience rather than a college degree, which she lacked, qualified her for the job. As a Black Community Developer, Mother turned into a social advocate second to none. Plus, Mother came to see that ministering to all God's people became redemptive personally.

When I began my local church ministry in 1970, I followed my mother's example and based a large part of my ministry on serving others. In essence, the mantra Mother articulated when we were kids—"We don't have a lot of money, but you can serve"—found its place in my ministry. Of course, our practice of service ministry has been expressed differently—mine primarily through priestly functions and hers as a social prophet.

Philander Smith College

When I headed to Philander Smith College in Little Rock, Arkansas, Mama was thrilled. It was a Black College supported by The United Methodist Church. More important, before starting her family, Mother had attended Philander for one year. My acceptance affirmed a connection of which Mama was justly proud. Reverend D. H. E. Harris, my grandfather, was said to be the first black trustee on the Board of Trustees of Philander Smith College. Although Mama wanted me to attend Philander Smith, when I arrived on campus I had no scholarship, no car, and no money from home that could be spared for my education. Though empty-handed, I was filled with dreams of becoming the first of my siblings to graduate from college, the hopes and aspirations of the black folk in my local church, and the notion that "all things are possible with God."

My conflict with Mama over "being a preacher" resulted in my decision to major in premed. Although my diploma from Philander Smith eventually read Bachelor of Science in Biology, all my hours of study did not yield a high grade point average. Stone wall after academic stone wall bruised my hopes, dreams, and selfhood. However, I stubbornly refused to change my major.

As graduation neared in May 1968, I knew that no medical school would or should accept me. My academic record showed little promise for a distinguished career in medicine. Ironically, my work-study job on campus did. I was assigned to the Religious Life Office of the Media Offices. Working in the area of religious life on campus, and at the campus church (that is, historic Wesley Church), I thrived and excelled. By the end of my first year, I received the 1967 Distinguished Service Award. Beyond the normal routine of acclimating to campus life that included activities such as pledging Alpha Phi Alpha fraternity and singing in the college choir, my most enjoyable moments came from the sense of accomplishment I received from working on projects in the Religious Life Office. A growing resonance of ministry as a vocation began to compete with my expressed goal, namely, becoming a doctor. Then, Mama died on May 26, 1967, and from that day until I answered the call to ministry in the summer of 1968, I felt an internal struggle to choose ministry over medicine. The protracted struggle remained until I said yes to God's call. As Jesus' death and resurrection transformed the world, so did Mama's dying transform me. Her death broke down my resistance. And I was faced with a reality shaped by my resistance that Mama did not live to see her dream come true. "But such is the stuff of life."

Heading North to Seminary

Although I applied for admission to Gammon Theological Seminary in Atlanta, Georgia, I cannot remember receiving a confirmation letter. Yet I still have a copy of my completed application. During the summer of 1968, Garrett Theological Seminary issued a call for admission to black students with the promise of financial support. I applied and was accepted. Truly, I am one of the blessed ones. Academically speaking, I had no significant justification for being there. If I made it at Garrett, it would take a miracle. I arrived at Garrett safe and sound but alone. God had brought me through one more wilderness experience. Another more daunting than the one just faced loomed ahead. In faith, Mother had put her twenty-two-year-old son on a bus bound for Chicago with a used footlocker holding my wardrobe, a radio from my college days, and less than one hundred dollars in my pockets. After a nineteen-hour trip, I arrived in Chicago—a city of strangers. Alone, I was buoyed by the faith and the hope of a living mother and the haunting call of a departed grandmother and burdened with the expectation to succeed for myself, my family, and black folk in general. I had been cast into another wilderness. Just as quickly as I began the trek through the wilderness called Garrett, an oasis appeared.

Ervin Smith, Gessel Berry, and Herbert Martin arrived the same year. Herb had a student appointment at Sherman Church in Evanston, and he invited me to attend. Less than two weeks after my arrival, I had a church home, a few African American student colleagues, and the prospect of learning from a black professor on faculty, Edsel A. Ammons. Within the first quarter of our arrival, the four of us made financial, curriculum, and faculty demands on the administration on behalf of black folk. We faced reprisals from other students and faculty for these acts of liberation. But God made a way somehow. Even as we formed the Garrett Black Seminarians to espouse our cause, the subsequent conflict and striving equipped us for ministry in ways we could not perceive at the time. For me this included myocarditis striking me down, my comprehensive exams not yielding the quality expected, and the writing of my dissertation that plodded rather than galloped along. When it seemed that I might not regain my health, overcome my academic challenges, or write a quality document, God, who makes all things possible, brought me through. By the time I graduated, God had become a comforter, a provider of financial resources, a presence in times of struggle, a restorer of failed hopes, a rescuer from serious illness, and a resource for learning and living up to the academic standards of Garrett. I no longer needed the words and stories of Mother and Mama to convince me of the reality of God. In my journey, God had become real to me. God performed miracle after miracle for, through, and in me.

Ordination

I was ordained deacon in the Northern Illinois Conference in 1970. My classmates Herbert Martin and Gessel Berry were ordained as well. With ordination, my journey as a local church pastor began—a journey that required huge adjustments on my part. Seeing the St. Luke facility on the South Side of Chicago for the first time was stunning. Less than two hundred folk were on the rolls. More important, it was the first time I had seen a church with bars on the windows and gates that locked across the doors. There was more. Row after row of often crime-infested public housing rose nineteen to twenty stories high, a block away. Though I remained stoic on the outside, fear gripped me inside. Had the Cabinet or the Lord really sent me to pastor in such a strange land? What could a young man from Arkansas do here? God showed me.

First, doubts about my chosen vocation no longer dogged my heels. God had called me. Hence, I was determined to be an effective local church pastor and serve the Black Church all the days of my ministry. Second, this African American congregation (a remnant of historic

St. Mark) took a rookie under its wing and trained him to be a faithful pastor. Third, most of the fears that I had about ministering to folk in the so-called dangerous community vanished in the process of serving them. All this happened with God's help. A number of years after my departure, St. Luke merged with Hartzell UMC. Nevertheless, the members and ministry of St. Luke had a powerful impact on me. This church on the South Side of Chicago became "holy ground" and remains so even today. Ordination as an elder in 1978 and earning a doctorate degree from Garrett-Evangelical Seminary in 1979 crushed my dream of serving the Black Church all the days of my life. Despite my protestations, the bishop moved me to a white church.

The Journey Continued

Good news, God's news. As with Jonah, God decided that he would use me to serve people and communities beyond my own. Hence, my joy and servanthood have been enhanced and strengthened in serving Christ and the whole church. I was privileged to serve as the pastor of Broadway UMC in Rockford, Illinois, as a member of the CCOM Program Staff from October 1, 1982, to June 30, 1990, and as Aurora District Superintendent from 1990 to 1996 in the Northern Illinois Conference. Subsequently, I was elected to the episcopacy in July of 1996. Before my current assignment in the Michigan Area in 2004, I served the Ohio East Area of The United Methodist Church from 1996 to 2004.

Section Two

On Spiritual
Leadership

PRAYER LIFE AND LEADERSHIP

Edsel A. Ammons

There are seldom times in the life of the church more full of opportunity for exploration and discovery in matters of spiritual formation, both personal and ecclesiastical, or for inquiry into the ground of our faith or reflection on the demands of a life of discipleship than the current era in history. In such a time as this of holy confluence when you yearn after God's presence and truth, God's offer of both through divine grace is a miracle almost beyond words. And its reality is apparent, at least in part, in the decision of three United Methodist bishops to consider how their own lives of faith and ministry have been inspired by God and given form that has enabled them to meet the demands of leadership that the office of bishop has required of them. It is safe to say that both inspiration and formation point to a disciplined and continuing devotion to the practice of prayer.

"Prayer life" is an abbreviated way to speak of a faith practice that is normative and unapologetic. Another way is to think of it as "living prayerfully" or in ways that literally sing of a life in direct and immediate relationship between creator and creature, in which the language of the relationship is personal and gracious and enduring. It speaks of much more than the occasional recitation of religious verse that may or may not be spoken at prescribed moments during the day, often characterized by brevity and repetition. Indeed, prayer life suggests *a way of life*, often without verbal expression, that is committed essentially to the quiet or silent speech or meditation of heart and soul.

Reference to "prayer life" or to "living prayerfully" brings to mind two words that are foundational: *attitude* and *habit*. The first is the prism through which we reflect on the unfolding events of the day and which determines, in considerable measure, what influence our faith perspectives may have on the shape of those events. To judge a situation "in a prayerful attitude," therefore, assures a view of it that is more than casual or informed by the latest gossip. Rather, it foretells a strong inclination to examine emerging circumstances and their developments in the light of a higher truth, which, for Christians, is the truth of the gospel of Jesus Christ. Nor does this imply starting from a predetermined or literal interpretation of Scripture, the error common to fundamentalist evangelicalism that leaves little room for the Holy Spirit to enable new awareness of old perceptions or to give birth to insight that is totally new or unexpected. Living in an attitude of prayer speaks of a graceful *habit* of the mind.

The second of the two words that are foundational to "prayer life" or to "living prayerfully" is *habit*. Attitude alone cannot remain sufficiently determined or focused apart from behavioral change or renewal. This is affirmed by Jesus in the memorable New Testament passage: "Neither do you put new wine into old wine-skins; if you do, the skins burst, and then the wine runs out and the skins are spoilt. No, you put new wine into fresh skins; then both are preserved" (Matt 9:17 NEB). And the point is again made by Jesus in his rebuke to the crowd seeking his blessing: "You vipers' brood! Who warned you to escape from the coming retribution? Then prove your repentance [your yearning to be better] by the fruit it bears" (Luke 3:7-8 NEB). Thus, the claim of new life in faith demands *evidence* of it that is clear and measurable, that is, done often enough and in a manner that is broadly acceptable.

The church speaks of such demonstration as "ritual" or "liturgy" and shapes its time in worship and its life of witness beyond worship accordingly. This is not to suggest that the habits of worship or of any other efforts by congregations and their leadership are necessarily identical. They are not, of course, and may vary as much as the people involved. But while these habits are varied and often radically different, the church does express itself with predictable regularity in word, in song, and in its prayers led by clergy or other leadership. Moreover, the garments often worn by leaders of congregational ritual were, and still are, called *habits*.

Two words, *attitude* and *habit*. What implications are there in them for those among us who are "set apart" by election and consecration to serve as bishops of the church? I begin by calling on a memory, still quite vivid, of a particular moment during a meeting with the district superintendents of the last annual conference over which I presided. It was customary for us to open our meetings by sharing information about the families of preachers and other leaders, followed by a brief time of worship, and then to conclude with a prayer by the bishop. One day before I began to pray, a superintendent asked me to say a brief word about my own prayer life, how has it grown from simple bedtime petitions to a passionate address to God that speaks to the heart of those who have heard me pray and, obviously, to the heart of the one who prays. The request was without a quick or easy reply. And for a few seconds, I did not answer as I awaited the inspiration of the Holy Spirit to help me decide the best way to respond. I said, at last, that my prayers are the fruit of a life "that has sought refuge in God, who enables me to survive the devastation of a culture that considers persons who look like me (having darker skin color) to be of lesser value." There was quiet as no noticeable reaction followed my observation. They had heard it before from "my kind of folk." And then one of them asked the question that may have been in the minds of several: "But tell us, Bishop, what is it that happens to you when you pray? We sense something remarkably different about you that is more than the words and phrases that we hear; something that in those few moments infuses the room with a powerful Presence with whom you seem engaged in a most intimate way." What I offered, with some embarrassment, and which they seemed to accept, was my confession that, when I begin to pray, "I imagine myself standing outside of myself, beyond limitations of flesh and circumstance, in total surrender to the One who gives life and who, in Christ, redeems life. It is in that time of radical self-denial that a prayer, summoned from deep within the soul, happens. And from that moment—that improbable moment of divine-human encounter—the prayer becomes conversation with the Almighty that is natural and authentic and compelling."

This unique episode in the busy schedule of a bishop and his Cabinet colleagues lingers in my memory. It came to mind again as I read, in an article by Diana Butler Bass, words by Thomas Merton: "Prayer is then not just a formula of words, or a series of desires springing up in the heart—it is the orientation of our whole body, mind and spirit to God in silence, attention, and adoration. All good meditative prayer is a conversion of our entire self to God." Recalling the special time with district superintendents, as I do occasionally, has informed my reflections concerning episcopal leadership in particular, and leadership in the church in general.

When elected bishop, one brings into the office an enormous range of experience and awareness of the life and work of the church in the world. The elaborate process of selection and election makes this fact quite apparent. But what becomes quickly apparent is that no one comes into the office with sufficient preparation for the multitude of responsibilities awaiting his or her arrival and episcopal judgment. A "crash course" in training often helps but only in modest degree. It is a frenzied time of exhausting adjustments when experience and knowledge previously gained simply do not suffice. Colleagues and friends can and will help, if their help is sought. But the help that brought me from "a mighty long way" and made it possible to survive the demands of each day in the new office was the prayers that filled my day (indeed, that made my day!) and calmed my anxious spirit.

And here I return to what I suggested earlier, namely, that life possessed by an attitude of prayer is blessed with extraordinary powers of perception about life and the nature of the world because of its focus on God who is sovereign over both. It is an attitude or view of things that equips us with the capacity to shape ideas, to make comparative judgments, and to risk coming to decision even when the truth is known only in part or not at all. Such thought and decision begin with the One who is the way and the truth, which is why Saint Paul urges Jesus' disciples to "*pray without ceasing*" (1 Thess 5:17 KJV, emphasis mine) or to "never stop praying. Be thankful, whatever the circumstances may be" (JBP). Prayer refines and strengthens our dedication to lofty and worthy objectives otherwise often neglected.

In The United Methodist Church, which rewrites its *Book of Discipline* and doctrine with considerable regularity, perspective is crucial to understanding the meaning and determining the shape of its ministries and its institutional systems. This has particular bearing on the work of bishops who are the chief arbiters or interpreters of Law and Doctrine and who must give leadership in such matters, especially at times of dispute or disagreement. Episcopal leaders who are known for the quality of their prayers (called "praying bishops" by some people) are held in high respect by many across the church who sense the influence of their prayerful ways as the church shapes attitudes and ministries. Prayer serves to form them and to enable the offer of themselves as a "living sacrifice, dedicated and fit for his acceptance," as good stewardship determines that they must do (Rom 12:1 NEB). In other words, what prayer offers as personal benefit to the one who "prays without ceasing" eventually benefits the entire church through the enriched life and leadership of the person. Where this leads concerning bishops of the church is rather easily perceived.

In strongest terms, it calls upon bishops to commit to the habit that gives depth and power to their leadership—the habit of prayer that is more than casual or occasional—far more than simply the exercise of a routine that comes with office and status. Episcopacy that remembers the legacy of its birth in John and Charles Wesley and, ultimately, in Jesus, senses the wisdom and value of the *disciplined* practice of faith. Second only to the Bible, *The Book of Discipline* (less now, perhaps, than in the past) has directed Methodism in the work of its ministry. In a world of widespread disorder or disarray, the church seeks order and leaders who can facilitate such order in the stewardship of its life. Methodism's founders knew that in the absence of an orderly and ordered practice of its liturgy and life, its effectiveness would be short-lived and without power of spirit to make a difference. The brothers John and Charles Wesley, for instance, practiced Holy Communion regularly, even daily communion. Yet Charles asks:

> Why is the faithful seed decreased,
> The life of God extinct and dead?
> The daily sacrifice is ceased,
> And charity to heaven is fled.

The highly regarded Rabbi Abraham Joshua Heschel speaks the same hope for the preservation of historic memory and related habit: "Only [one] who is an heir is qualified to be a pioneer." These prophetic words speak to a generation that is marked by decreasing respect for Christian or ecclesiastical tradition. It is solid counsel to United Methodism, which often seems wearied by or indifferent to its own history as a "people of the Book" (which includes both Bible and *Discipline*) as it pursues new or simply different views on the church's faith and its practices. In a time of confusion or unsettlement about either, the role of the bishop in providing clarity is increasingly crucial. And his or her leadership needs the grounding and the enrichment of mind and spirit that the unceasing practice of prayer can enable.

Finally, it serves us well to remember that the world in which the bishop "lives and moves and has his [or her] being" is filled with a plethora of relationships that are influenced by the prayerful manner of his or her leadership in and beyond the church. A question, which points to a very special category of relationships, is the one that asks, How is the bishop at home? Meaning, what are his or her presumptions regarding the Area Office? How does he or she relate to staff associates who want to feel the care of others who serve at Area headquarters? How does he or she live with and among clergy and laity who are partners in the ministries of the Area? How is he or she with spouse (if married) and children?

The Area Office can become simply a "place for the conduct of business," or it can be a source and center for holy imagining and facilitation of creative ministry. Much depends on the bishop, who is frequently away from the office attending one of many meetings. If, however, the bishop is inspired to consider headquarters personnel as more than "hirelings" and, instead, as gifted colaborers in the ministry of Christ's church, grace will prevail as will the capacity to maintain a focus on the task even when vision is blurred and the way ahead is uncertain. In that context, the bishop's leadership is less CEO—big desk and narrow spirit—and more pastor-shepherd.

An even greater challenge to episcopal leadership is relations with clergy and laity. What become immediately apparent are the several important ways clergy matters "land on the bishop's desk." Primary among them is the appointment-making function, which takes up the majority of the bishop's time and emotional energy. Indeed, the responsibility for the annual assignment of preachers to congregations and other work will surely teach the bishop how to pray and the necessity for doing so! This helps explain the special value of Cabinet meetings when the bishop and the district superintendents are together in prayer and meditation to "make appointments" and, in a somewhat limited way, evaluate continuing fitness for ministry of clergy.

Increasingly, leadership in prayer and meditation has become the most viable way for the bishop to engage the life and witness of the laity except, perhaps, in congregational visitations and educational experiences. Certain changes in the definition of the laity have prompted them to assume greater responsibility for advocating on their own behalf and for developing the programs that they consider vital to their ministries. Such change in relationship and focus has resulted in the emergence of a generation of intuitive and creative laypersons who continue the tradition of a strong laity with whom clergy conference leadership remains in critical and prayerful dialogue.

Most of the stories about the family life of bishops and, in fact, about the clergy home in general have mercifully been written. Certainly, much can be said about the impact upon and neglect of the family due to the demands of the episcopal office. Again, this is a place where everyone benefits from a prayer regimen that is constant and devotional. It is a fact, of course, that at the time of election, most episcopal families are without small (or even teenage) children. The burden, therefore, that conscience lays on the absent parent of children is far less. The quality of a prayerful existence becomes the task of mature adults who will need to be as deliberate in planning it as they are in shaping every other phase of their lives together.

LEADERSHIP

Ernest S. Lyght

Leadership is a popular topic both in secular circles and among religious societies of every denominational affiliation. Corporations want a CEO who will lead them to financial success. Local churches say they want pastors who will provide leadership that yields effectiveness in ministry and mission. Annual conferences say they want a bishop who will lead the conference in the development of a meaningful vision and the effective implementation of ministry and mission. This book, although informed by leadership in the corporate sector, is not intended to be a treatise on corporate leadership. As bishops of The United Methodist Church, we are concerned about effective pastoral leadership. For practical reasons, corporate leadership ultimately must be distinguished from pastoral leadership. Bishops, therefore, should exemplify the qualities of dynamic leadership.

What is leadership? Is there a difference between *corporate* and *pastoral* leadership? In short, every group, whether corporate or religious, wants its leadership to be effective. The following is a brief examination of basic leadership and the distinctions between corporate leadership and pastoral leadership.

There are numerous and diverse definitions of leadership. *The Reader's Digest Great Encyclopedic Dictionary* defines leadership as: (1) the position or office of a leader; (2) the ability to lead; or (3) a group of leaders. The focus of this definition is on the position of a leader. Little or no attention is given to the purpose and the characteristics of effective leadership.

Robert E. Quinn describes a leader as one who brings about transformation in the organization. The workers are able to mobilize around an action plan that is aligned with the organization's core values. Such a transformational leader sets an example for all the workers, who in some way emulate the leader's discipline and commitment.

An early leadership guru, Peter F. Drucker, described a leader as an *effective executive*. He argued that effectiveness is a leadership dynamic that can be learned by an executive. The need to learn effectiveness is based on the premise that it is the express task of an executive to be effective. What is effectiveness? Simply stated, effectiveness is *self-discipline*.

The effective executive or leader, according to Drucker, demonstrates some mastery of five dynamics:

1. To be more effective, the leader must learn how to manage time well.
2. The effective leader is able not only to articulate the vision but also to stay focused on the vision at all times.
3. The effective leader is a learner who strives to be more productive, building on personal strengths in others as well as the leader's strengths.
4. As a time manager, the effective leader is able to establish the appropriate priorities or discern *first things first*.
5. The effective executive or leader learns to make good decisions through acquired knowledge, learned skills, and experiences gained over time.

Effective leaders, according to Jim Collins, are adept at getting the right people into the organization. Such leaders are ambitious, yet steeped in humility. These leaders move the organization from *good* to *great*. They understand business thinking, yet they are able to transcend such thinking as they build the organization. To be sure, a leader is one who influences other people in a positive manner. Leadership, then, has to do with the ability to influence others. The effective leader must be a person of good character and integrity. An effective leader is trustworthy and builds trust among colleagues. This leader has a vision and is able to communicate his or her vision. Leaders like this must know themselves as well as they know their organization. These characteristics are needed by both corporate and pastoral leaders.

Several years ago, a bishops' learning group spent several weeks studying the theory of constraints. This learning group included both United Methodist bishops and several General Agency General Secretaries. The group, made up of laity and clergy, grappled with the theory of constraints as applied to industry. The theory of constraints has to do with *input*, *throughput*, and *output* in a manufacturing process. When output is not up to par, or production is down, the managers begin to look for the constraints that are restricting the final output or production. What keeps the manufacturing plant or an organization from achieving more of its stated goals? This learning group cautiously applied the theory of constraints to The United Methodist Church. The stated mission (goal) of The United Methodist Church is to make disciples of Jesus Christ. The group probed the issue of what is needed for The United Methodist Church in its many local congregations to make disciples of Jesus Christ, its stated goal. They prayerfully concluded that The United Methodist Church needs pastors who are spiritual leaders on the Path with other spiritual leaders. This dynamic is a key distinction between corporate leaders and church leaders.

Effective leaders are needed at every level of The United Methodist Church. A local church needs a pastor who can lead the congregation to grow in Jesus Christ and to engage in vital ministry and mission. A district benefits from a district superintendent who has a vision and is able to lead congregations in developing their unique vision that in turn leads them toward spirituality and wholeness. Bishops also need to provide visionary leadership for the annual conferences, where districts and local congregations can fulfill the church's mission: *making disciples of Jesus Christ for the transformation of the world.*

It is necessary for The United Methodist Church to stay focused on its mission in a world that needs transformation. The world can be transformed only by transformed clergy and laypeople. Here we are talking about spiritual transformation. The local church, therefore, needs a leader who is a spiritual leader on the Path with other spiritual leaders. Local churches and annual conferences need leaders who will enable the particular community to achieve more of its mission, making disciples of Jesus Christ.

The Pilgrim Disciple's Journey

Christian disciples, regardless of their denominational affiliation, are on a journey that lasts for a lifetime for the serious and committed pilgrim. The journey is linear, yet it is circular as well. It is linear in the sense that there are stops along the way. These stops or markers are the seasons of the Christian year. These stops provide an opportunity for the pilgrim disciple to pause for a time of reflection and fresh beginning. The pilgrim disciple's journey is also circular, enabling one to revisit the prior stops. Annually, the Christian church celebrates the seasons of the Christian year. The years of one's life pass, but the markers are repeated. One might say that the journey is also progressive, with a variety of personal growth possibilities along the way. The pilgrim disciple's journey is one of learning about Jesus Christ and growing in Jesus Christ. In our learning and growing, it is imperative for a pilgrim disciple to seize every opportunity to experience God's fresh beginnings in a creative way. The beginning of a new year is one such opportunity, when viewed from the perspective of John Wesley. At the beginning of each new year, Wesley invited the members of the societies to renew their covenant with God. The new year, of course, is God's fresh beginning. This fresh beginning at the start of a new year provides an opportunity for the pilgrim disciple to renew his or her covenant with God.

John Wesley's Covenant Prayer declares that the pilgrim disciple belongs to God and not to himself or herself. We are subject to God's will, not our own. The Covenant is ratified in heaven, not on earth. The pilgrim disciple is on the Path with Jesus, and the spiritual journey lasts for a lifetime. Nelle Morton proposes that *the journey is home*, which is also the title of her autobiography. Pilgrim disciples are seeking to make heaven their home, but they also are striving for perfection in their earthly home. We constantly miss the mark, however, and stray from the Path in our relationship with God. So, we need other stops and markers in addition to the new year.

One such significant marker is Christmas, which is preceded by the Advent journey of preparation and making room for Jesus in one's life. At Christmas we encounter the Jesus of Nazareth, who came into the world bearing grace and truth in abundance. We pause; yes, we stop and clear some of the clutter from our busy lives to ensure that there is plenty of good room for Jesus in our hearts and our daily living. Another significant marker is Easter, which is preceded by the Lenten journey, which is a time to engage in a fasting of the heart. A fasting of the heart is not about giving up trivial things, such as candy, ice cream, or coffee for Lent. A fasting of the heart has to do with coming to grips with that which serves as a chasm between God and oneself, where the focus is on self and not God. We encounter the risen Lord in the Easter event. In other words, like Mary Magdalene, we meet Jesus in person. After her personal encounter with Jesus, Mary Magdalene said, "I have seen the Lord" (John 20:18 NEB). We come face-to-face with God's resurrection power. We are able to confront life in our daily living in a fresh way because we acknowledge in no uncertain terms that we serve a Savior who lives in our hearts and is in the world right beside us. We need to be reminded of this awesome reality on a regular basis in our public worship time and during our personal meditation time.

During Pentecost, another major marker on the pilgrim disciple's spiritual journey, there is a sense that the disciples of Jesus were promoted (not graduated) to a new field of service. They stopped off at the Upper Room and spent a considerable amount of quality time in conversation with God. It was Jesus who had taught them how to pray. Jesus also modeled a constant prayer life for them in his daily living. God bathed them with the Holy Spirit and gave them the confidence and the ability to do the work of ministry on their own. The key to their new ministry was the fact that they did their acts of ministry solely in the name of Jesus. That reality was God's fresh beginning in their lives.

The Disciples Were Called to Be Spiritual Leaders

Jesus called the disciples to follow him and to learn how to fish for people. These called men were commercial fishermen, and they knew their craft: fishing for fish. They did not know anything about fishing for people. Jesus had to train them. Jesus had to prepare them for a new way of living and being. Jesus entered into the process of preparing the disciples for spiritual leadership by introducing them to new ideas about the kingdom of God. He exemplified a holy life in their presence.

Before they could launch into their new ministry, the disciples of Jesus had to overcome their fears. Their first fear was for their own lives. Would they be identified as followers of Jesus and crucified like he was? Their second fear was that they would be a failure without Jesus by their side. Their renewed faith, in the aftermath of the Easter event, displaced their fears. When the day of Pentecost came and went, they realized that Jesus was with them. Momentarily, they had forgotten that Jesus had promised to be with them and to go with them to all of their places of ministry. Jesus kept his promise and continues to maintain his promise to the faithful. It is important to remember that the disciples participated in three years of in-service training with Jesus. This experience was in fact a spiritual leadership academy. They learned how to be spiritual leaders in doing the work of ministry. What did they learn? First, they learned how to pray. Second, they learned to believe in themselves, because Jesus forgave their betrayals and denials and trusted them. Third, they learned that the effectiveness of their ministry was not couched in their talents or their lack of talents. The effectiveness of their ministry was rooted and grounded in the name of Jesus. The folks in the early church, the Acts church, relied not on themselves but on Jesus, who empowered them through the power and presence of the Holy Spirit.

The second chapter of Acts tells a story that illustrates spiritual leadership. As was customary, one day at the hour of prayer, Peter and John were making their way to the Temple. They met a man who had a handicapping condition from birth. People would place him at the gate of the Temple called the Beautiful Gate. In that location he was able to beg for alms from the worshipers who were entering the Temple. Naturally, when he saw Peter and John entering the Temple, he asked them for alms. Peter and John both looked at the man intently. Note that they did not look through him, nor did they look away from him. Instead, they invited the man to look at them. The man looked at them, fully expecting to receive a donation from them, but they surprised him. With full eye contact, Peter told the man that he did not have any money to give him. Peter told the man that he would share with him what he had, namely, Jesus, and invited him *in the name of Jesus Christ of Nazareth* to stand up and walk. Peter grasped the man with his right hand, and the man's feet and ankles were made strong. This healing ministry was accomplished by responding to a ministry need in the name of Jesus.

The Spiritual Path

Jesus of Nazareth was on a spiritual journey, and he invited the disciples to unite with him and follow him on the journey. One day while doing ministry with his disciples, Jesus told the disciples that they should not let their hearts be troubled. Instead they should believe in God and believe in him, Jesus. He told them that there are many dwelling places in God's house. This statement was based on the premise that Jesus was going ahead of them to prepare a place for them. Jesus made this promise: "And if I go and prepare a place for you, I will come again and will take you to myself, so that where I am, there you may be also" (John 14:3). Jesus then asserted that they knew the place where he was going. Thomas reminded Jesus that they did not know where he was going. Since they did not know the path chosen by Jesus, Thomas pondered as to how they could know the way. As the pilgrim disciple journeys forward on the spiritual Path with Jesus, the assurance is that through faith we rely on the power of the Holy Spirit to lead us and to sustain us on the Path. When we do the work of ministry, we do it in the name of Jesus. The church and its ministry are solely about Jesus, the Light of the World. We are not alone on the journey. We are partners with God and with one another.

It was then that Jesus shared the itinerary, the route, the path for the disciples. Jesus answered Thomas: "I am the way, and the truth, and the life. No one comes to the Father except through me" (John 14:6). Jesus is the Path. Jesus reminded the disciples and reminds us that if we know Jesus, we will know the Father too. In knowing Jesus, the disciples knew the Father and had seen him. When Jesus declared that he was the way, it was a clear indication that the pilgrim disciple must travel with Jesus, even as the disciples traveled with Jesus. While traveling with Jesus, they built a personal relationship with him over time. They also developed a personal relationship with one another. They learned to live in community, sharing all things in common as each person had a need. Living in community, the disciples came to understand that there is a need to care for someone other than oneself. No longer were they fishing for fish; they were becoming fishers of people. While growing in their own discipleship, they were learning to make disciples of Jesus Christ.

As the disciples learned the art of making disciples, they were learning about the new ideas that Jesus introduced to them, for he was not only the way but also the truth. Jesus was pregnant with grace and truth, and he shared these gifts with all who listened. Jesus would take the old ideas and teachings of the Bible and transform them into principles for kingdom living. As Jesus taught kingdom living, he also taught the people that kingdom living on earth was a prerequisite to life in the Father's house. Jesus wanted the disciples to love him and keep his commandments: love God, love yourself, and love your neighbor. Jesus told his disciples that they would receive the spirit of truth, if they loved him and kept his commandments. The spirit of truth is the Advocate who would be with them forever.

The understanding that Jesus is the life suggests that following Jesus requires the pilgrim disciple to change, live a new life, and follow the teachings of Jesus. The Apostle Paul underwent a dramatic change in his life that converted him from persecuting Christians to a life of proclaiming Christ. After his conversion experience, Paul gave his whole life to

Christ and the ministry of making disciples of Jesus Christ. John Wesley, the founder of Methodism, wanted to live a more holy life. As he struggled to be more holy in his Christian and ministerial endeavors, he struggled to stay on the Spiritual Path with Jesus until his Aldersgate experience, when his heart was strangely warmed. For Paul, life in Christ was to become a new creation. Life in Christ for John Wesley was a matter of holiness and striving to go on to perfection.

Life on the Spiritual Path is not easy. Like Jesus, spiritual leaders do not journey alone but stay on the Path with other spiritual leaders, laity, and clergy. Notice that Jesus was never a loner in his earthly ministry. Jesus called twelve disciples and traveled about with them, and together they engaged in ministry and mission. Jesus, however, did step aside for quiet meditation and conversation with God. These private moments provided time for personal renewal and relaxation, which are key ingredients of spiritual growth over time. The disciples and Jesus lived together, learned together, did the work of ministry together, and grew together in their relationship with one another and with God.

The Spiritual Leader

Jesus was a spiritual leader. The Gospel of John describes Jesus as one who came into the world full of *grace* and *truth*. Even as a teenager, Jesus began to show signs of spiritual leadership when he went to the synagogue and engaged the learned religious leaders in questions and answers. He was on the Path that God had given him to traverse and invited others to walk with him. Jesus said to Thomas, "I am the way, and the truth, and the life" (John 14:6). Jesus is the way to the Father, and there is no other way. Jesus invites us to join him on the way. Come! Follow me. I am the door. I am the Good Shepherd. Spiritual leaders over the centuries have responded to this invitation with affirmation.

Who is a spiritual leader? A spiritual leader is one who is on the Path with other spiritual leaders. Spiritual leaders are persons who have said yes to God's claim on their lives. Spiritual leaders are pilgrim disciples who are striving daily to grow in Jesus Christ. Spiritual leaders are persons who are going through a constant spiritual metamorphosis. These leaders are of such spiritual character that other people see Christ in them and desire to follow their spiritual leadership. Spiritual leaders know that they cannot abandon the Path.

John Wesley's Spiritual Principles

John Wesley bequeathed to Methodism three basic principles, known as the General Rules, that guide one's life on the Spiritual Path as a Methodist pilgrim disciple. The idea is to show evidence of one's desire for salvation:

1. *By doing no harm.* The pilgrim disciple seeks to avoid evil of every kind.
2. *By doing good.* The disciple always seeks to be kind and merciful to all people and in every situation.
3. *By attending upon all the ordinances of God.* The ordinances of God include public worship, Holy Communion, family and private prayer, Bible study, and fasting or abstinence.

John Wesley set forth one basic requirement for admission into the Methodist societies: "a desire to flee from the wrath to come, and to be saved from their sins."

John Wesley and the Means of Grace

Further insight about the Spiritual Path is gained by examining John Wesley's means of grace. Wesley identified five means of grace as evident in the life of Jesus. He understood the means of grace to be "outward signs, words, or actions" that were ordained by God. These means were ordinary and normal channels through which God could convey to humankind preventing, justifying, or sanctifying grace. It is important to remember, as previously noted, that Jesus was on the Spiritual Path during his earthly ministry, and spiritual formation was an important part of his spiritual life. There are five important means of grace for Wesley:

1. *The Lord's Supper or Holy Communion.* He believed that the sacrament of Holy Communion should be celebrated as often as possible or desired. In The United Methodist Church, there is a growing trend toward celebrating the Lord's Supper more often than once every first Sunday. God enriches us, indeed nourishes us, through the Lord's Supper.
2. *Prayer, both private and public.* Wesley believed that not only should a Christian pray frequently, but prayers should not be brief. The challenge is to set aside an appointed time(s) for prayer. Prayer is our

conversation with God, and it opens our hearts and minds to the voice of God, indeed, the will of God. Prayer enables a disciple to discern God's deepest yearning for oneself. Not only was prayer an essential part of Christian living for John Wesley, it was the most important means of grace. The pilgrim disciple, who is on the Path, must review and examine his or her prayer life on a regular basis.

3. *Fasting, which can take a variety of forms.* Wesley firmly believed that fasting would help a person become more disciplined and steadfast in his or her spiritual life. Fasting not only requires discipline, it demands patience and practice. Typically, fasting is construed as giving up something for a specified period of time; however, it is much more than this. Poet Ann Weems offers a more profound understanding of fasting. She invites the pilgrim disciple to examine fasting in light of the Isaiah 58 text in her poem "Giving Up for Lent."

4. *Regular study of Scripture.* Scripture should be studied on a private basis and in small groups. For Wesley, Bible study was a daily practice. Wesley would make relevant notes as he read the Bible, poring over individual texts, chapters, and books. Those pilgrim disciples who journey on the Path profit from having a personal method for searching the Scriptures.

5. *Christian conference, which is conversation among pilgrim disciples.* Christian conversation is an integral part of community. It is perhaps the foundation of community. Community, of course, has to do with how we choose to live together as brothers and sisters in Christ Jesus.

Spiritual leaders strive to live by the General Rules, and they imbibe God's spirit through their participation in the means of grace. That is what it means to be on the Spiritual Path.

The Pastoral Nature of Spiritual Leadership

There are five dynamic characteristics that constitute the pastoral nature of spiritual leadership. People who engage in pastoral ministry manifest these characteristics in the conduct of their ministry. These characteristics, however, are not limited to pastoral ministry in a local church setting, but these characteristics can also be found among people who serve in extension ministries and as district superintendents and bishops. These characteristics are *prayer, presence, practice, passion,* and *proclamation.*

Prayer has already been mentioned as an essential and integral part of spiritual leadership. The spiritual leader spends a considerable amount of time in prayer and meditation. A key element in prayer is the art of listening, listening to God. Prayer time provides an opportunity for the person at prayer to listen to and encounter God's intimate thoughts. Disciplined prayer requires the one praying to stop, look, and listen. One must stop the normal routine and step aside from life's business and engage in conversation with God. Honest prayer facilitates the opportunity for looking at oneself as a matter of personal observation. Prayer requires the person praying to talk with God *and* to listen to God. Listening for any length of time is a difficult posture because the general preference is to tell God all about our troubles, forgetting that God already knows our troubles. The spiritual leader who learns to listen to God is better able to listen to all of God's people who are participants in a particular ministry. Jesus invites us to listen to the lambs, especially when they are crying.

Presence is a matter of holiness. When Moses stopped to determine why the burning bush had not been consumed by the flames that had engulfed it, he discovered that he was in the presence of God. He also was informed that he was standing on holy ground. Because he was standing on holy ground in the presence of God, God told him to remove his shoes. Spiritual leaders need to take off their shoes on a frequent basis, because they need to stand on holy ground and tarry in God's presence. United Methodists covenant with the church and promise to uphold it by their presence, among other things (that is, prayers, gifts, and service). Presence in a local congregation provides an opportunity for the worshiper to be nurtured spiritually and educationally. Fellowship is also a part of our spiritual formation. When we leave the sanctuary, we go out into the world to serve God's people, and then we return to the sanctuary to be nurtured again and again. Another part of presence is the regular participation in the Eucharist, yet another opportunity to be in God's presence. Perhaps William D. Longstaff says it best in his hymn, "Take Time to Be Holy."

> Take time to be holy, speak oft with thy Lord;
> abide in him always, and feed on his word.
> Make friends of God's children, help those who are weak,
> forgetting in nothing his blessing to seek.

Spiritual leaders practice a ministry of presence with God and with God's people.

Another area of concern to the spiritual leader is the matter of *practice*. What do we do with our spiritual gifts? What service do we render with our spiritual gifts? The Apostle Paul in 1 Corinthians 12 talks about the varieties of gifts, service, and activities. According to Paul, the spiritual gifts are wisdom, knowledge, faith, healing, the working of miracles, prophecy, the discernment of spirits, a variety of tongues, and the interpretation of tongues. All pilgrim disciples have a gift or gifts from God; however, a person may not be aware of all of his or her gifts. Appropriate gift inventories are available to help an interested person discover his or her spiritual gifts. Known spiritual gifts can be developed further and newly discovered spiritual gifts can be cultivated as a part of one's spiritual formation and continuing service in the life of a worshiping congregation. We are gifted by God in order to use our gifts for the work of ministry and mission, which is a spiritual practice.

In addition, spiritual leaders are driven and sustained on the Path by a *passion* for the gospel of Jesus Christ. Our passion is rooted in our obedience to God's will. Martin Luther King, Jr., was driven and sustained by his desire to do God's will. During the months prior to his assassination, it no longer mattered what might happen to him; King simply wanted to do God's will. He was not concerned about longevity because of his passion for doing God's will. King was committed to achieving freedom and equality for all people, so he returned to Memphis to lead a second demonstration on behalf of striking city sanitation workers. Our passion is grounded in the cross of Jesus Christ, for it is at the cross that we meet Jesus in all of his passion (that is, triumph, betrayal, and execution). Our power is amplified and transformed by the power of the resurrection. The Apostle Paul came to know Jesus in the passion of the cross and was transformed by God's resurrection power. Paul says in the twilight of his life, "I have fought the good fight, I have finished the race, I have kept the faith" (2 Tim 4:7). This verse reflects Paul's passion for the work of ministry and mission. His focus was on Jesus Christ, so Paul always preached about a crucified Christ. He lived life with the passion of one who knew in practical terms that Jesus died on the cross for him and his sins.

Finally, the spiritual leader knows the story of salvation, strives to live the story, and tells the story through *proclamation*. The story is the good news of salvation through Jesus Christ. It is not so much our story, but it

54

is the story of what Jesus Christ is doing in our world and in our lives. The pilgrim disciple who is on the Path loves to tell the story of Jesus and his love. We tell the story so that others can hear it and make their own personal response.

The Wesleyan Essentials of Spiritual Leadership

John Wesley wanted spiritual leaders to focus on the personal salvation of the people with whom they held a spiritual relationship. It was in the classes that the leader could determine whether or not the class members were *working out their own salvation*. The leader had a responsibility to inquire of the class members how their souls were prospering. Also, the leader would give advice to, reprove, comfort, and exhort the members. The leader was responsible for the temporal and the spiritual welfare of the society.

The Spiritual Test of Spiritual Leadership

Effective leadership is not about having the right answers to all of the questions arising. Quite the contrary, it is essential for leaders to pose the right questions in all situations. All of God's children have spiritual questions. Spiritual leaders help pilgrim disciples articulate their spiritual questions. They also articulate their own spiritual questions in the face of the crises in life, personal and public. The ability to help others voice their spiritual questions is the spiritual test of spiritual leadership.

THE BISHOP AS SPIRITUAL LEADER

Jonathan D. Keaton

In his letters to Titus and Timothy, Paul paints a picture of an ideal if not a spiritual bishop. The bishop must live a disciplined life (avoid arrogance, anger, and greed and be self-controlled, hospitable, and good, Titus 1:5-9). Paul's epistle to Timothy emphasizes similar themes. For instance, the bishop must be above reproach, manage his house well, not be a lover of money, not be a recent convert, and possess the respect of church and society (1 Tim 3:1-7). These qualities are implicit in paragraphs 414.1 and 414.2 of *The Book of Discipline—2004*. They define the general boundaries for exercising spiritual leadership as a bishop in the church, in the world, and in relationships. Below, I approach my subject from a functional perspective. By this, I mean those aspects of my episcopacy that receive *most* of my time, energy, and attention. What follows are varying snapshots of my work as a member of the Council of Bishops, as the presider during annual conference(s), as the superintending leader of a Cabinet(s), as one who builds relationships with local churches, and as an administrator particularly as it relates to answering letters.

Council of Bishops

In my tenth year as a bishop, my roles on the council are twofold. First, I strive to be accountable to the faith community known as the Council of Bishops (COB). Second, I work at building relationships with the whole council while sharing a closer fellowship with a few. Issues and personalities can and do fracture, strain, and test the unity of the council, having an impact on relationships and teamwork. To be a faithful part of the council requires love, respect, patience, speaking out, and prayer.

Within the council, I serve on the appointed committees and participate in the plenary sessions, worship, and other work assignments. Depending on the perspective, the COB is a laboratory for learning.

Lessons are available in every aspect of the church's life in the example and personality of active and retired bishops. This includes the spiritual life of a bishop. Beyond worship, members of the council attend to their spiritual needs and challenges best in small Covenant Groups. Studying the Bible, discussing issues that strain COB unity, praying together, sharing of personal and family struggles in confidence enable all council members to strengthen the link between themselves and God. When the Ebony Bishops meet at the COB, more connections are made in the light of our minority status in the church. The opportunity to learn from those who have been there is a rich supply of spiritual food and nurture for active Ebony Bishops.

Without naming names, a small number of colleagues on the COB make it possible for this bishop to serve faithfully. To lean on and be a support, to pray on behalf of and to be prayed for, to challenge and to be challenged in utmost humility by friends who want to see the best use of my gifts on behalf of Christ and his church are gifts of God I do not richly deserve but certainly covet.

My travels throughout the connection involve several areas of responsibility. The yearly training event for District Superintendents / Directors of Connectional Ministries (DS/DCMs) takes place at Lake Junaluska, North Carolina. My work includes teaching, preaching, and offering advice and counsel to those who seek me out for extended conversation. In addition, Ebony Bishops spend one dinner hour with black DS/DCMs. Networking, discussing issues of concern raised by persons appointed to serve in a majority, and praying are the order of the day.

Chairing Strengthening the Black Church for the Twenty-first Century (SBC21)—an initiative of the 2004 General Conference—requires much prayer and work to build up the fortunes of black folk diminishing in the UMC. SBC21 continues to make a difference in the lives of black churches. As far as participants in the SBC21 ministry are concerned, this initiative keeps "hope alive." This bishop is God-convicted about SBC21 and will give it his last ounce of devotion. Why? Serving as the chairperson of SBC21 puts me in the forefront of advocating for the Black Church, particularly for its growth and survival. Connecting strong African American churches with partner churches who want to grow spiritually and numerically is working. If black folk are to flourish once more in the UMC, support and advocacy must continue through initiatives like SBC21, support by National Black

Methodists for Church Renewal (BMCR), the Ebony Bishops, and the whole church.

Foundational to my work across the connections is leading Spiritual Growth Studies in the Schools of Christian Mission sponsored by the United Methodist Women. Fifteen years prior to and the ten years since my election, I have led spiritual growth studies. Delineating how these studies influence my ministry as a bishop is nearly impossible. Clearly, my leadership role and thought process reflect a deeper understanding and sensitivity to mission and ministry due to the privilege of serving in this teaching role.

Presiding at Annual Conference

As Sunday service is the time and place where the pastor is most visible to the people gathered, so is the annual conference for the bishop. Expectations are enormous, especially with regard to presiding, preaching/worship, and the articulation of a vision to inspire and strengthen the mission and ministry of the church.

Reading, writing, meditation, prayer, discernment, and a retreat preceding annual conference are the foundation of my preparation for annual conference. Without them, I could not sustain the leadership skills required of the bishop. Reading and understanding conference legislation, applying Robert's Rules and God's rules, remaining alert, vigilant, and helpful in a sometime contentious environment require the resources of God and humankind. More important is the leadership needed to help local churches accomplish their mission in ministry. More and more, I embrace the statement of Father Theodore Hesburgh (president emeritus of Notre Dame) on visionary leadership as essential: "The very essence of leadership is that you have to have vision. You can't blow an uncertain trumpet." As a vision statement, "Making disciples for the transformation of the world" shapes my episcopacy in a large way.

Occasionally, anomalies occur during annual conference. In my former area of responsibility, one memory stands out. After I appointed a woman to a local church, a delegation from the congregation traveled to the site of annual conference to confront me between sessions. For the next half hour, the air was filled with angry questions and answers. None of my answers were helpful to them, and they demanded that I withdraw the appointment. No amount of explaining the appointment process, sharing the gifts and graces of the female pastor, or exhibiting a calm demeanor could diminish their anger. Distinctly, I remember one woman standing toe-to-toe with me noting her displeasure and promising that the church would not financially support my appointment. Upon informing the group I could stay no longer, they reluctantly allowed me to pass. I did not change the appointment, but I do know that the spirit of the living God carried in that hour. Members of the annual conference had gathered, listening to every word spoken between me and the disaffected group. Observing closely what I said, how I said it, and my behavior displayed with an angry group from a local church allowed the bystanders to note whether I would take the high road or the low road. By the grace of God, I took the former.

All in all, my approach to annual conference is to prepare prayerfully as best I can and leave the rest to God.

Cabinet

In Cabinet and Extended Cabinet meetings, four areas receive the bulk of my spiritual leadership: worship, appointment-making, bishops' concerns, and pastoral care. Worship in community is foundational. What the word says regarding our "collegial style of leadership" and personal journeys shapes our ministry. The singing of songs, the praying of prayers, the reading of Scripture, preaching and sermon feedback truly become a "means of grace" to us. Also, monthly Communion nourishes the life of the Cabinet. The nature of Christ's mission and sacrifice puts in perspective the trials and tribulations of superintending. What we do requires a focus on God, not us.

Bishop Linda Lee, my predecessor, left a committee in my hands that emphasizes God's concerns. Lee formed a Prayer Team during her episcopacy. When I came to the Michigan Area, the Prayer Team wanted to know if I desired to continue. So, I have learned to pray for the work of the conference in a collegial framework outside the COB and the Cabinet. Mostly, the Prayer Team was formed to keep the spiritual leadership in order. To reap the maximum benefit from this small community, I have had to become vulnerable anew. Yet I am learning to grow with a Prayer Team dedicated to keeping the bishop on task with his prayer life. For this, I give God thanks and praise.

Appointments

Research, discernment, prayer, and a consciousness for social justice are especially helpful in the process of deploying pastors and their families. Congregations tend to rise and fall based on the work of the appointed pastor. Regardless of the consultation means of grace employed, some appointments never work. When such failures occur, all parties involved feel a sense of humiliation, frustration, and possibly helplessness. Knowing that, why pray? Why seek God's assistance? Success aside, we believe that God leads and acts through all circumstances. We believe that God acts through a praying community— that God chooses to do something special through the giftedness of a particular leader—that God operates on a plane not fully discernible to a cabinet, bishop, local church, or pastor. For those appointments that turn out to be disasters, God still moves the church forward. Crosses and losses have the capacity to "increase the wisdom" of the Cabinet and bishop in the future deployment of pastors. Quite frankly, this bishop trusts that most appointments are right for a season, notwithstanding length of tenure. We note this reality in the appointment of Saul as the first king of Israel. Saul's kingship is rather short. God unseats him because of spiritual malfeasance (1 Sam 13:7b-15a). At bottom, appointment-making contains a paradoxical element. What may happen to a church or pastor is beyond human comprehension. By faith, we live into the process of appointment-making.

That said, justice issues do complicate the appointment process. Appointing women pastors and ethnic minority persons continues to plague the process. In other words, some churches do not want to accept them. Ethnicity that differs from the majority in a congregation, language, scriptural beliefs that God does not call women to preach, and so on are cited as legitimate rationale for not cooperating with the bishop's appointment. If the bishop wants to appoint such persons to major churches, the challenge is even greater. Cabinet members are not immune from such thinking. In the process of consultation, bishops become aware of persons on their Cabinet unable to entertain the appointment of women and ethnic persons to major fields of labor. When this situation occurs, the bishop must be grounded in knowledge of the situation and be in touch with God regarding the appointment.

Bishop's Concerns

Here, the bishop lays out a litany of concerns before the Cabinet. More important, it is my time for "discipling" members of the Cabinet. For example, we may review an excerpt from one of Wesley's sermons, discuss the moral implications of a Judicial Council decision, or continue reflecting on the text used in the Cabinet devotions. Sometimes the Cabinet takes on the nature of class meetings. Superintendents give an account of how they are leading the District in making and equipping disciples for Jesus Christ. More and more, the bishop seeks to move them away from simply fulfilling the roles of administration and institutional maintenance. What they see as God's vision for the District, what they are doing to facilitate it, how they are using the leadership of clergy and laity under their supervision are primary elements of their evaluation. Also, a portion of the concerns above relates to the ability of each superintendent to motivate, equip, and teach the District about the responsibilities and demands of stewardship and evangelism.

Pastoral Care

Whatever the gifts and graces I possess for the episcopacy, they count for nothing if my leadership does not include pastoral care. The finest sermons, lectures, tidbits of advice fall by the wayside if the sheep and shepherds under my care languish because no pastoral care exists. Although Jesus' visit to Peter's mother-in-law is a small part of the gospel, it is no small thing. First, she is healed. Second, she meets Christ, and they have a meal together. Third, Peter's mother-in-law learns about this Messiah to whom her son-in-law has committed his life. Fourth, undoubtedly, Peter's mother-in-law and wife become supporters of Peter and his ministry because of one single act of pastoral care. The same phenomenon influences our ministry. If nothing else, spiritual leadership involving genuine caring is ministry and reflects the gospel of Jesus Christ.

The late Daisy Spurlin taught me this valuable lesson in my first church. She insisted that we visit the sick and shut-in monthly. Persons I visited shared the history of the church, gave me their tithes and offerings, praised God that I, their pastor, cared for them, blessed me for serving them Communion, and affirmed the value of pastoral care. A recent experience in my episcopacy confirmed this truth. One of my superintendents went on Renewal Leave for the summer and became deathly ill. By phone, I contacted his wife and prayed for both of them. Instead of simply telling her husband about my call, she took the phone into intensive care and played the message for her husband. To this day, her husband has spoken to me often about what that prayer meant. In his hour of need, the superintendent received care, love, and inspiration from God's word from the voice of his bishop delivered over a cell phone.

Ministry of Presence

An aspect of strengthening local congregations and building relationships means a ministry of presence. As such, congregations have direct contact with me in three venues: preaching, attending a special local church event, and occasionally meeting with PPR (Parish-Pastor Relations) Committees and concerned groups to consult and interpret the bishop's perspective regarding a major conflict or concern.

There is no substitute for "being there." Presence makes real the leadership concerns of the bishop. Priorities that I espouse become flesh in human interaction. Whether it's preaching, conversation at a meal, questions and answers, or a simple handshake or prayer, a closer relationship is established. And the bishop becomes known to congregations as a real person. As Christ becomes known to his disciples in "the breaking of bread," so presence helps congregations fill in the blanks regarding their bishop.

In worship settings and at funerals, clergy and laity catch a glimpse of the spiritual depth of the bishop. What I say about the sudden passing of a pastor by heart attack or suicide, how I address the ongoing trials and tribulations of a church over homosexuality, what I do to help churches with diminishing numbers and stewardship, how I treat conservative and liberal constituencies in the church reflect my God talk and beliefs. Presence is the ongoing lament of many people in the Michigan Area who live in the Upper Peninsula (UP). Clergy and laity alike express feelings of abandonment because the conference—symbolized in the office of the bishop—is an eight-hour drive. Whether it is a visit to the UP or a church in Lansing, the response of the people to my visit is gratitude! In other words, a bishop who makes time in his or her busy schedule to hear and interact with folks on the front lines of ministry inspires and encourages the flock immeasurably. I know. Words spoken to me, letters in my drawer, tapes in my head, baptisms, communion services, counseling sessions, funerals attended, hospital visits made, gifts directly given, and prayers prayed bear witness to the power of presence. Haunting me still are the words Mary and Martha speak to our Lord, who arrives in Bethany after the death of their brother Lazarus saying, "If you had been here, my brother would not have died" (John 11:21). Clergy and laity hunger for opportunities to engage the bishop. What the bishop learns from these visits deepens relationships and enhances the decision-making capability of the Cabinet and the bishop.

Letters

In spite of a somewhat common Episcopal opinion, Letters do not, if given time, answer themselves. The fact that you have no decisive answer to give does not mean that there is no such thing as common courtesy. If the bishop himself fails in courtesy, how can he expect it from others?

Sacerdos Et Pontifex is a book written by a retired Catholic bishop at the request of a new bishop-elect seeking advice about the episcopate. The advice found in the quote above demonstrates another venue where a bishop has opportunity to exercise spiritual leadership. I refer less to the matter of answering letters and more to the way a bishop these days must respond to letters crossing one's desk.

Letters come to the bishop with a menagerie of complaints. Some letters accuse the bishop of allowing liberal causes to run the ministry of the church. Writers point to the promotion of a man-centered gospel, gender neutrality, support for abortion relativism, and so on. Others decry the bishop's lack of support for the policies of George Bush, particularly in Iraq. Often, the writers threaten to withhold the payment of apportionments unless bishops, the conference, or the church get it right. In response to nonpayment of apportionments, I remind persons who are upset that the *Book of Discipline* does not support the withholding of apportionments—that two wrongs do not make a right. Usually, though, that response falls on deaf ears.

Still other writers try to trap the bishop with questions, allege that the bishop is killing the church, or say they want to ban the Council of Bishops from speaking to the church on the matter of homosexuality unless a certain perspective is affirmed. Month after month, wave after wave of such letters come in. If a bishop is not careful, he or she may choose not to answer such letters (not appropriate) or feel a smoldering desire to lash out at accusers (even less appropriate). To answer such letters, one must be constantly in prayer and reflection and ask the fundamental question that may seem trite for some: What would Jesus do? We know. Typically, our Lord would answer his critics without revenge, put-down, name-calling, invective, anger, or lingering bitterness. All complaints would find their place in the ministry of reconciliation—a reconciliation seeking to bring the kingdom on earth as it is in heaven. This is my approach to letters accusing the bishop of seemingly everything under the sun. On the other hand, letters come to the bishop as a balm in Gilead. They evoke words like thank you; thank you, Jesus; and God is good.

Functionally Speaking

Surveying the landscape of the roles emphasized in the Episcopal snapshots, a couple of observations are in order. First, teaching, preaching, pastoral care, relationships, and writing claim an enormous amount of time. Prophetic roles that evidence themselves in public demonstrations, letter-writing campaigns, signing petitions, contacting my congressmen on a number of social issues are not plentiful. Most of my advocacy work finds its focus in the African American church, community, and family, especially through the denominational committee on Strengthening the Black Church for the Twenty-first Century. Although I am accountable to the whole church, life has shaped and formed me in such a way that the particular concerns and needs of my community are ever lying on my conscience and shoulders.

The overwhelming responsibilities of the office and the need to focus one's ministry on a few priorities mean that the bishop must look to and employ others to extend his or her ministry (that is, to represent the bishop on occasion). At bottom, providing spiritual leadership mirrors a response given life by the late Thurgood Marshall upon his retirement. Asked about his legacy or what he wanted people to say about him, Marshall shared the following, "Say, he did the best he could with what he had." That is what I am trying to do in the fulfillment of my collegial responsibility to lead the church as a spiritual leader.

Section Three

SERMONS

MAKING GENTLE THE LIFE OF THE WORLD

Edsel A. Ammons

First Reading: Romans 12:1-16a
Second Reading: John 17:1, 4-6, 9-11, 14-23
Let us pray: "Let the words of my mouth and the meditations of our
hearts be acceptable in thy sight, O Lord, our rock and
our redeemer." **Amen.**

My friends, I want to start by saying to you what a colleague, Bishop
King of Kentucky, usually says to a congregation: "Good morning,
beautiful people!" And now a story.

A number of years ago, I read in a Columbus, Ohio, newspaper an article about thirty-seven freed slaves. In 1849, they traveled by foot and
oxcart four hundred miles over mountains from Madison County,
Virginia, to the southern Ohio town of Burlington. Their descendants
still live there and struggle to keep alive the memory of the thirty-seven
who had longed for a place that would accept them and their aspirations.

The heart of this story is the man who made their triumph of human
resolve possible. He was a wealthy Virginia plantation owner who, in his
will, provided that, at his death, the thirty-seven slaves would be freed
and given enough money to make a fresh start in a free territory. There,
in a tiny corner of a nation torn by hatred and violence and diabolical
oppression, was a rare and shining act of hospitality between people
thought to be destined by social custom and national policy to be enemies
forever.

The account of one man's human gesture introduces my message to
you on this special day. Like many of you, I am concerned about our society's drift toward increasing hostility and violence causing people to be
fearful and defensive, to cling anxiously to their personal space, and to

look at the world around them with suspicion as if expecting some enemy to appear suddenly and do them harm. It is a climate of foreboding that threatens our well-being, a worrisome sign of the loss of a sense of security and community. And it is a phenomenon that has produced overworked lawyers and judges and mountains of litigation aimed at those who are thought to have violated our space or our person.

There did seem to be at one time a greater willingness to settle disputes among neighbors with as little fuss and injury as possible. The object was to preserve community. Now we seem obsessed with motivations that are much less charitable, more rigid, and at the expense of community. This may explain in part why, for many people, at least, there is little regard for the more excellent way of which Scripture speaks in Jesus' summary statement of the law in which the whole of life, personal and social, holds together. While I do not deny the importance of civil and criminal statutes and of those who defend and interpret them in our collective interests, I am more convinced of the primacy of the law to which Jesus points if our embattled society is to make its promised journey from hostility to hospitality. In his book *Reaching Out*, the late Henri Nouwen stated that "the vocation which ought to claim all of us, whether advocates of statutory or of ecclesiastical law, is to convert *hostis* into *hospes*—to turn the enemy into a guest, to create the safe and fearless space (where brotherhood and sisterhood) can be formed and fully experienced."

The Bible underscores the value of hospitality in any serious search for personal and social spirituality. Remember when Abraham received three strangers at Mamre and offered them water, bread, and a fine, tender calf, they revealed themselves to him as the Lord announcing that Sarah, his wife, would give birth to a son (Gen 18:1-15). Or when the two travelers to Emmaus invited the stranger who had joined them on the road to be their guest for the night, he made himself known in the breaking of the bread as their Lord and Savior (Luke 24:13-35). In another passage, the absence of regard for strangers—or inhospitality toward them—caused the destruction of Sodom and Gomorrah. Not questionable sexual preference, as some argue, but social meanness was their undoing (Genesis 19). And we can imagine what emotional anguish must have been experienced by the innkeeper who could find no space in his establishment for a young and pregnant Mary and her worried husband, Joseph (Luke 2:7).

Such biblical stories suggest that hospitality is a virtue that is central to the well-being of our life together and needs new emphasis in our day in view of the evidence of growing estrangement between us and others and the selfish pursuit of personal gain at the neighbor's expense. In its broadest sense, hospitality is an attitude toward others which is critical to the rebirth of our fractured communities into ones held together by a warm and heartfelt graciousness toward neighbor and stranger and where hope can be experienced in the middle of crying cities, broken aspirations, desperate parents and their children, and threatened and anxious churches.

Saint Paul's words signal his high regard for community. "By the mercies of God," he exclaims in his letter to the Romans, the people of Christ are to live together as a body that functions harmoniously—held together not by their desire for conformity but by a spirit born of the love of Christ, which overcomes all that separates and divides. Having "gifts that differ," let us use them discreetly and with care; "let love be genuine," practice hospitality, "do not be haughty" or conceited "but associate with the lowly" (Romans 12). The burning core of the apostle's teaching is that we who are of many kinds and races are cut from a single garment and are called to come into one community, which is united in devotion to Christ. Clearly, a community such as Paul envisioned is not the product of human inventiveness; it is a creature of God's divine initiative, the fruit of the covenant by which God became our God and we became God's people and sisters and brothers to one another. In a boisterously beautiful way, the British hymn writer, Brian Wren, speaks this same truth in his song "When Minds and Bodies Meet as One."

On January 16, we mark the birthday anniversary of Martin Luther King, Jr., who in an equally boisterous or forceful manner, witnessed to a consuming passion for community as Shalom, a passion that has been shaped in the crucible of a way of life where oppression is the constant companion of his people. Thought by many to be an impractical visionary, Martin Luther King believed to his death that this nation was ordained of God to be the guardian of sacred ideals in this awful age in which people believe their doubts and doubt their beliefs. And he challenged us to devote ourselves to a cause that would test the last full measure of that devotion. The simple folk, who had never really counted before, saw in him one who understood their sufferings. The sophisticated responded to him as the good man who could bring the nation to the fulfillment of its potential—a potential, according to the president of a theological seminary, that is in "desperate need of leaders who are committed to the values of inclusion, tolerance, respect, love, and justice, thus, the values of the Gospel"—to spiritual maturity about which we say much but often do little.

Fulfillment of the nation's promise requires more. It requires dramatic new behavior to enable emergence of a hospitable life together—the free and safe space we all desire. In an age torn by inequities, that means giving first consideration to the forgotten and hurting people who are victims of life's tragedies and cruelties and to whatever efforts are necessary to create lasting and caring relationships with them. (Again, hear Paul's words: live in harmony; associate with the lowly.) How often have we said it ourselves that the measure of a nation's greatness is how it cares for the poor? Martin Luther King, Jr., was careful to keep us aware of this mandate of our faith, as he was careful to insist that obedience to it lays upon us the responsibility to draw ethical distinctions and raise probing moral questions in order to find ways of defining reality in a manner that exceeds our limits and ultimately blesses us. His was the hope to move us toward the goal of a society of gracious hospitality by learning to think beyond our culture's obvious fascination for "practical" people, that is, beyond our romance with the "realist," and dare to align ourselves with dreamers.

Martin Luther King, Jr., was compelled by a view of life, which sounded impractical to many—like a dream, if you please. It was and is far more than that. And because of it, this nation has come closer to the righteous of heart and soul for which our foreparents and we have prayed. Of course, King and other visionaries like him knew the risks they faced and that not all the aspirations of mind and soul become realities, that we must seek to reach beyond self-interest and affirm values that inspire compassion and make neighbors of strangers and friends of enemies.

Which leads to the conclusion that, for the sake of the hospitality that is absent in much of our life today, we must follow Martin Luther King's example and commit ourselves to the way of reconciliation. Love, the law that ultimately matters most, must become the norm and style of our lives. The morality of our faith demands nothing less. Brother Martin did not hesitate to declare that this is what Jesus Christ demonstrated. In the heat of controversy over the hard issues of the day, it is easy to forget the central truth of our faith that the future itself demands that we love neighbor and enemy, urges us to prefer hospitality and to disdain hostility. (The sign over the Reba Place Church in South Evanston reads, "We pray for the world, for our nation, and for enemies.") Speaking at a gathering in Indianapolis on the night Martin Luther King was assassinated, Robert Kennedy (soon to be the victim of an assassin's bullet himself) spoke eloquent words:

> What we need in the United States is not division; what we need in the United States is not hatred; what we need in the United States is not violence and lawlessness, but is love and wisdom, and compassion [and hospitality] toward . . . those who still suffer. . . . Let us dedicate ourselves to what the Greeks wrote so many years ago: "to tame the savageness of [humankind] and make gentle the life of this world."

That remains the challenge of our life together called as we are by a faith

> that will not shrink
> Though pressed by every foe,
> That will not tremble on the brink
> Of any earthly woe!

Reflection on the life of our martyred brother reveals to us the course we must follow if we wish to make his vision a reality—to get from the dream to the community it implies. Making gentle the life of the world, disciples who will transform the world (a stated purpose of The United Methodist Church), will require a renewal of heart and mind, a disavowal of the disposition and ugly evils of bigotry and hatred, which build the walls that separate people and spoil their dreams. That was what he meant when, in one of his most memorable moments, King averred that only love could eliminate hate. With unforgettable clarity, he saw the evil that poisons our national life, and that may be ever deeper now as we move from benign neglect to careless abandonment of the poor and the rejected. Personal bias has led to national policies, which, by their very design, can only fracture community and make enemies of neighbors. To turn things around and move us toward a future that is kinder and gentler requires more than political rhetoric and maneuvering. It will require a conversion of mind and soul evoked by the hope that claimed Martin Luther King, Jr.

King was a prophet of a realized hope who spoke with great power and delight of the joy that comes in the morning and followed that with his familiar challenge to us to find hope in despair. He called for a new ethic, for the kind of action that the change of an evil system will demand. Therefore, he and his friends sang songs and they walked and they prayed and they endured beatings and jail and other indignities believing, as he helped them believe, that if they continued the struggle, then one day love and community would win out over hatred.

His was a faith having within it a fulfillment motif. Like the Christ of the gospel, King never doubted the power of God and of good to triumph over evil. Hallelujah! Words from the lips of Martin Luther King, Jr., had the ring of holy majesty. A humble preacher and a prophet of peace and justice had a fetching way of turning a phrase! He had been to the mountaintop, had looked over and seen a company of angels, and felt anew the touch of his Master's Spirit, and he became someone that no sinful act could silence. And he lives on, Martin does, in the minds and hearts and the politics of countless millions who refuse to think of him as yesterday's headlines. We shall forever be in his debt, who shook the foundations of this land, as we endeavor to make his vision more than a dream for the sake of our own souls and that of a nation that needs to rediscover the purpose of its special place in making gentle the life of this world. Merciful God, let it be so. Amen.

HIT THE ROAD

Ernest S. Lyght

Then the woman left her water jar and went back to the city. She said to the people, "Come and see a man who told me everything I have ever done! He cannot be the Messiah, can he?"
(John 4:28-29)

And many more believed because of his word. They said to the woman, "It is no longer because of what you said that we believe, for we have heard for ourselves, and we know that this is truly the Savior of the world."
(John 4:41-42)

We have gathered here today in the name of Jesus, because we know something about that name. Hymn writers Gloria and William Gaither said:

> Jesus, Jesus, Jesus!
> There's just something about that name!

We are tarrying here this morning to worship God and to celebrate the sacrament of Holy Communion, in remembrance that Jesus gave his life for our sins. It is in the name of Jesus that we have the victory. All of us here today know the name of Jesus. But do we know the power in his name?

One day Jesus met a woman who did not know his name. Jesus learned that the Pharisees had heard the rumor that Jesus "is making and baptizing more disciples than John" (John 4:1). It was on this occasion that Jesus decided to hit the road. He left Judea and started back to Galilee, making his way through Samaria. Tired from his long journey, Jesus stopped at Jacob's well to rest, while his disciples went to Sychar, a Samaritan village, to buy food.

The Scripture passage notes the fact that it was noon. Noon, of course, is the time of day when the sun is at its fullest. It is a time that one often tries to avoid, to protect oneself from the sun's brilliant rays. In biblical times, noon was often a time for rest. It was also the hour of prayer. It was the time of grace. In this story, it is the time of day that we find Jesus sitting by Jacob's well, cooling off and resting his weary feet.

Jacob's well was a good place for Jesus and the disciples to rest because Jacob's well would provide them with good water. The well was fed by underground springs, and its water was fresh and cool. When the water in a well was moving and not from a cistern, the ancients called it "living water."

Jesus encountered and engaged a Samaritan woman who came to the well to draw water. Without any introduction, Jesus said to her, "Give me a drink." Obviously taken by surprise, the Samaritan woman said to him, "How is it that you, a Jew, ask a drink of me, a woman of Samaria?"

Now let us pause and check up on some of the pertinent details of this cross-cultural encounter. First, Jesus was alone with the woman because the disciples were gathering their lunch. Second, in that time, Jews did not share things in common with Samaritans. Third, it is implied that no self-respecting Jewish man would ask a Samaritan woman for anything, much less something so personal, yet common, as a drink of water. Nevertheless, Jesus asked the woman for a drink of water.

Jesus responds to the woman's query in a spiritual manner that literally stunned her, while at the same time arresting her undivided attention. He lets her know that she obviously does not know the gift of God, Jesus. Neither does she know that she is in conversation with Jesus at Jacob's well. The point is that if she had known, she would have asked him and he would have given her "living water."

Brothers and sisters, she did not know Jesus, not yet. In like fashion there are many people in our neighborhoods who do not know Jesus. They have no idea that Jesus can give them "living water." Why, because no one has shared that message with them in a convincing way.

The woman, realizing the depth of the well and noticing that Jesus had no bucket, wanted to know where Jesus would get this "living water." Not knowing who Jesus was, the woman was not able to understand the import of his response. She was thinking about bottled springwater whereas Jesus was talking about *eternal life*. Now, a bottle of chilled springwater is good, but it is not eternal life.

There was a major gap in communication here. The woman was not yet "feeling" Jesus, yet Jesus was "feeling" the emptiness of her spirit. Jesus wanted to know if she was "feeling" him. Jesus explained to the woman that the water from Jacob's well would not quench her thirst. He shared with her the reality that "those who drink of the water that I will give them will never be thirsty. The water that I will give will become in them a spring of water gushing up to eternal life" (v. 14). The woman asked Jesus to give her some of this water to quench her thirst and allow her to cancel her standing order for bottled springwater. Without realizing it, she was asking for salvation.

Listen to the response that Jesus gave to the woman. In a curious way, Jesus told the woman to hit the road. He said, "Go, call your husband, and come back." Remember that it was twelve noon, the heat of the day. No other women were at the well. Perhaps the Samaritan woman came at this time to avoid the condescending stares of the neighborhood women. She was probably the subject of local gossip on more than one occasion. Figuratively speaking, she wore the scarlet "A" reminiscent of Hester Prynne in Nathaniel Hawthorne's *Scarlet Letter.* The "A" stood for adultery and sin.

The woman readily admitted that she did not have a husband. Jesus noted that she had told the truth and told her that she not only had had five husbands, but "the one you have now is not your husband."

After this exchange the woman thought that Jesus was a prophet. Jesus continued the conversation about worship and salvation. He said, "God is spirit, and those who worship him must worship in spirit and truth" (v. 24). Jesus wanted the Samaritan woman to know that the time was coming when what one is called will not matter. Where you go to worship will not matter.

What counts before God is who you are and the way you live. Your worship must engage your spirit in the pursuit of God's truth, Jesus (the way, the truth, and the life).

The woman mentioned her belief that the Messiah is coming, and he will proclaim all things when he comes. Jesus told her, "I am he, the one who is speaking to you" (v. 26).

It was then that the woman hit the road. She left her water jar and went back to the city.

She said to the people, "Come and see a man who told me everything I have ever done! He cannot be the Messiah, can he?" (v. 29). The people who heard her message hit the road so that they could see and hear Jesus for themselves.

I would like to think that the Samaritan woman seized the opportunity to stop by home and have a conversation with her live-in boyfriend. I suspect that she went home and told him that she had met Jesus, and she was no longer the same. I also hope that she seized the opportunity to sing to him in the words of the late Ray Charles, "Hit the road, Jack, and don't you come back no more." This fellow needed to go so that the woman could begin to live a transformed life in Jesus.

If there is someone who is blocking your relationship with Jesus, tell that person to hit the road. Then you can hit the road and spread the good news: "He told me everything that I have ever done."

What was on the mind of this Samaritan woman? First, she was guided by her genuine humility. Second, her spiritual eyes enabled her to discern the truth. Third, she had a good heart, and she hit the road in order to preach the good news. She was indeed one of the first evangelists.

Brothers and sisters of the West Virginia Annual Conference, I believe that Jesus wants each one of us to hit the road and share the good news.

When the disciples found Jesus engaged in conversation with the Samaritan woman, they were silent. Eventually, they urged Jesus to eat some food. He told them, "I have food to eat that you do not know about." The disciples did not think that someone had brought Jesus some food. Jesus said, "My food is to do the will of him who sent me and to complete his work" (v. 34).

Hit the Road, Friends. It's Harvest Time!

Remember the Scripture now: "Many Samaritans from that city believed in him because of the woman's testimony, 'He told me everything I have ever done.'"

At their request, Jesus tarried among the Samaritans for two days. Then Jesus hit the road so that he could share good news in other places. Many other people came to believe because of Jesus' word.

After this experience with Jesus, they said this to the woman: "It is no longer because of what you said that we believe, for we have heard for ourselves, and we know that this is truly the Savior of the World" (v. 42).

It's Harvest Time in the West Virginia Conference: Greenbrier District, Little Kanawha District, Midland South District, MonValley District, Northern District, Potomac Highlands, Southern District, Wesleyan District, Western District—let's hit the road! In the name of Jesus!

A TOUGH CALL

Jonathan D. Keaton

DS/DCM Training
Lake Junaluska, North Carolina
Monday, August 28, 2006
1 Samuel 3:1-20

God makes a tough call during the childhood of Jeremiah. Yahweh appoints Jeremiah as a prophet to the nations without his consent. Samuel receives a similar call as a youngster. Rehearsing some aspects of this biblical case study may help our new appointees place in context why they were drafted or called up to be a Director of Connectional Ministries or District Superintendent. Focus on the following: *Samuel's call to ministry is a tough call.* It is rooted in his mother's desire for children, rooted in preparation and God's call in the night, and rooted in high performance expectations.

First, **Samuel's call to ministry is rooted in his mother's desire for children.** Samuel's mother was named Hannah. She married Elkanah. Elkanah had another wife named Peninnah. Why? In those days, polygamy was legal. Elkanah was a God-fearing man. Annually, his family made the pilgrimage to Shiloh to worship, to praise God, to petition Yahweh for surcease regarding personal and national problems. At the time, Shiloh served as a Holy City long before David captured Jerusalem and made it the center of Judaic life. Three priests ran Shiloh, Eli, the chief priest, and his two sons, Hophni and Phinehas.

Tension filled the marital relationship between Elkanah, Hannah, and Peninnah. Elkanah and Peninnah had children. Hannah had none. To help Hannah deal with this void, Elkanah treated her extra special. For example, whenever they went to Shiloh, Elkanah gave Hannah a good portion of food and professed his love for her countless times. Nothing worked. However, Hannah's special treatment displeased Peninnah. So, she continually mocked Hannah because she had no children. Unable to contain her grief any longer, Hannah cried out to the Lord during one of her annual visits to the Temple in Shiloh. As Hannah cried and prayed, she made a bargain with God. If God granted her a son, Hannah promised to give him back to God.

Moved by Hannah's heartache and public sorrow—empowered by the spirit of God—Eli, the chief priest, told Hannah to "go in peace." He believed that God would answer her prayers. Eli's comments represented an about-face. When Hannah had entered the Temple initially, Eli thought she was drunk and upbraided her. But Hannah's grief had become so palpable and hurtful that it reduced her to mumbled prayers. After our dear sister took everything to God in prayer, a God thing happened. God gave her peace. And Hannah was sad no longer. She and Elkanah went home, conceived, and had their first child together. Against the tradition of naming the first son after dear old dad, Hannah named him Samuel. His name meant, "I asked of the Lord." God granted the request of Hannah.

As we notice, Hannah's bargain with God has major consequences. Finally, Hannah gets what she wants, a son. For three wonderful years, little Sam is hers to kiss, hug, feed, change, and cherish. For three years, little Sam is the apple of his father's eye, to play with, to hold, and to dream of a better future. Little Sam carries the bloodlines of the family, but he will not follow in his dad's footsteps. Elkanah is disappointed. The wife whom he loves intends to follow through on a promise made to God. She will give their son back to God. Hence, Samuel will not grow up with his brothers and sisters. They will not really know him. Any hope that Hannah will change her mind is dashed when Hannah bundles up three-year-old Samuel and heads for Shiloh with Elkanah in tow. They transport their son to Shiloh and prepare to leave him there. Is this child abandonment in the modern sense? No. For Samuel will be given over to one of the most responsible figures in Jewish society, the chief priest. What we observe is a mother being true to a bargain with God. Upon arrival, Hannah seeks an audience with Eli. She rehearses the story of her miraculous conception and the promise made to God and seeks Eli's blessing. Then Hannah offers a sacrifice and prays a prayer like the prayer of Mary upon learning of her favor with God. True to her promise, Hannah hands her baby over to Eli and departs with the testimony, "He is given to the Lord" (v. 28).

Coming to the church, walking on the streets, and dominating television screens are the Elkanahs and Hannahs of this world. They are hurting. Crosses and losses mark their lives. Lord, if you'll just bring my daughter home from Iraq, Iran, or Lebanon; if you'll bring my mom home from prison; Lord, if you'll help me get the right appointment, I'll do thus and so. Some of the hurting and bargainers with God may have parallels with those who lost loved ones in the Sago Coal Mine of West Virginia. In a three-hour period, they go from praising God to cursing God, from believing there is a God to wondering if there is a God who really hears and answers prayers or bargains of the heart. Yes, some of them are like Elkanah and Hannah. Finally, they have a child but cannot keep it. A bargain made with God in crisis stands in the way. Since Elkanah did not bargain with God, he probably belongs to a school of thought claiming that Samuel belongs to them. But Hannah objects. According to Hannah, Samuel belongs to God, pure and simple. God has been faithful; so must she. A mother's faithfulness to a promise made with God means parting with her one and only son.

Samuel's entrance into ministry is rooted in preparation and God's call in the night. Literally and figuratively, the decision of this mother set the stage for Samuel's call to ministry. Astute observers of biblical history will be motivated to inquire about Hannah's fundamental decision. Why did she bargain with God with the promise of giving up her only son? Other options were available. In the process of giving their sons back to God, the parents of John the Baptist and Jesus raised their sons at home. Both sons made incredible contributions to the world, then and now. What kept Hannah from training her child at home in the way he should go? Why had she made a different choice? Perhaps Hannah believed the method of ensuring that her son would serve God forever and the training required to attain it could best be done by others. Have not parents and sponsors sent their children away from home for specialized training down through the years? Have they not used convents, Olympic gyms, and tennis factories to train their children to be champions? For example, the parents of Maria Sharapova sent her to Florida from Russia as a little girl. They wanted her to become a tennis champion. Many parents would have refused to take such a risk. For better or worse, Maria's parents determined that Maria would be prepared for a future as a championship tennis player in a strange land. So far, their dream has paid off. In like manner, Hannah decided that her son would spend his life serving God. It paid off as well, but not without growth, maturation, and years of struggle.

Born in Ramah, Samuel is raised in Shiloh by his adoptive family. From a babe to a boy, from boyhood to manhood, the life and work of his adoptive father shaped the mind and spirit of Samuel. Samuel helped Eli and his two sons minister to pilgrims who came to offer sacrifices, pray, worship, and seek counsel from them. In addition, he had a privilege and responsibility few people had in Shiloh or anywhere else. Samuel worked in the sanctuary that housed the famous ark of the covenant. The ark held the stone tablets of Moses inscribed by the hands of God. More important, Jews believed that the ark of the covenant was the actual dwelling place of God. As Samuel worked, he worked in, through, and around the presence of the Lord. By all accounts, Samuel served well. The writer of the book of 1 Samuel said as much in 1 Samuel 2:26, "Now the boy Samuel continued to grow both in stature and in favor with the LORD and with the people." Luke probably borrowed from that line in 2:52 crafting the following: "And Jesus grew in wisdom and stature, and in favor with God and men" (NIV). As Samuel grew and developed in ministry, he fulfilled the very dream conceived by his mother. Although in Ramah, Hannah supported the journey of her son. Every time the family made its annual pilgrimage to Shiloh, Hannah brought her son a new liturgical robe to wear. And Hannah brought the love and prayers of a mother. Impressed by Hannah's commitment to the bargain made with God, Eli asked God to bless her with more children. And God did. Hannah had three more sons and two daughters.

Still, Samuel's life was no bed of roses. As Samuel matured in years, he wrestled with a glaring reality. Eli and his wife were not his biological parents. Imagine young Samuel asking his parents some tough questions during one of their annual visits to Shiloh. "Mom, why did you leave me here in Shiloh? Why can't I go home with you and Dad? My adoptive parents are nice; so are my brothers. I love my adoptive father, Eli. I don't want to live here anymore. I want to go home and play with my brothers and sisters. Is Ramah like Shiloh? Mama, please take me home with you." Shaken and perhaps brought to tears by the profound yearnings of her son, Hannah recalls her promise to God. "Son, I love you. I always will. But you cannot go home with me. Years ago, I could not have children. I wanted them desperately. So I pleaded with God for a son. If God gave me a son, I promised to give him back to God. That was you, Sam. You can't go home with us. I made a promise, and I must keep it. You belong to God first; then you belong to me. You must stay here." And stay Samuel did, "ministering to the LORD under Eli" until God called (1 Sam 3:1). And God called in the night.

After a long day of serving pilgrims in Shiloh, Eli and Samuel went to bed. Samuel just happened to lie down in the Temple near the ark of the Lord. Then God called his name, "Samuel! Samuel!" He jumped up and ran to Eli saying, "Here I am, for you called me." Eli denied it and sent Samuel back to bed. God called twice more. Eli responded as before except on the third call. Perceiving that God was calling young Samuel, the chief priest advised his young understudy to respond, "Speak, LORD; for thy servant heareth" (1 Sam 4:9 KJV). In other words, God—whom the faithful believed had his dwelling place in the ark of the covenant—came out of the box or spoke from the box in such a way that Eli and Samuel were convinced it was the God of Abraham, Isaac, and Jacob, of Deborah, Sarah, and Rachel.

Coming to the church, walking on the streets, and dominating television screens are the Elkanahs, Hannahs, Peninnahs, and their children. To the degree that they darken our doors or relate to us, they trust us with their religious growth and development. We must take every configuration of family under our wings, graft them into the family of faith, train them up in God's ways so that their gifts may be used to the glory of God. And if by chance we discern that God is calling a boy or a girl, a woman or a man, to ordained ministry, tell them. Help them discern the voice of God calling. Be a burning bush, a spirit-led preacher or a prophetic voice crying in the wilderness. Be a church member or family member, a friend or foe pointing out the indwelling of God. Be a bishop who dares to call reluctant pastors or surprised pastors to come up higher in the service of the church via the roles of DS and DCM. Dare to send them out on a new journey with the convicting words of Fanny J. Crosby ringing in their ears,

> I am thine, O Lord, I have heard thy voice,
> and it told thy love to me;
> but I long to rise in the arms of faith
> and be closer drawn to thee.

My opening sermon in West Michigan and Detroit Annual Conferences commenced with an earnest plea, "We need another conversion experience." My plea focused on the Great Commission, undergirded by two alarming facts. First, for the thirty-eighth straight year, The United Methodist Church has experienced a decline in its membership. Second, 43 percent of our churches in North America did not receive any new members on profession of faith in 2004. Let me add another fact mentioned in the July 28 edition of *Newscope*. We'll likely see a decrease in church school attendance as well. In the midst of a successful Wesleyan ministry that permeates the world, we have failed to attract enough folk to offset our losses from moves, transfers, or death. Because of this dilemma, more pressure has been placed on the whole church, especially those called out to lead. In short, our membership dilemma has produced a greater demand for clergy to live up to high performance expectations in ministry. **Likewise, Samuel's call to ministry is rooted in high performance expectations.**

Eli's roots are rich and distinguished. He is a Levite. According to the book of Numbers, priests from the house of Levi were chosen to serve God forever (Num 3:5-10). In their job description were tasks such as leading worship, administering sacrificial offerings, guarding the ark of the covenant, caring for the sanctuary, providing guidance during times of peace and war, leading spirit-filled lives, and exemplifying their obedience to God. Eli lives up to that great tradition most of the time. His sons do not. The New Oxford Annotated Bible refers to them as "scoundrels" (1 Sam 2:12). Hophni and Phinehas take for themselves portions of all sacrificial offerings belonging to God. They profane the altar of God and have their way with the women. Everybody knows about it, even Eli. Despite his sons' numerous indiscretions, Eli does not ask them to take a leave of absence, go to personal counseling or therapy, surrender their ministerial office, or remove them from office. When he does question their unethical behavior, it does not even rise to the level of a private reprimand. God has no such hang-ups. Steps are taken to remove Eli and his sons from their offices. *The Abingdon Bible Commentary* offers this perspective: "There is no such thing as a 'divine right' of priests, no 'apostolic succession' that cannot be broken. God calls a [person] to a task, to its duties and its privileges . . . but if the duties are neglected, the privileges are withdrawn."

In responding to God's call in the night, Samuel is confronted with some sobering facts. First, God had called him into ministry. Samuel knew not where the call would lead nor the specific roles he would play. Second, Samuel learned that God was upset with Eli. He failed to restrain his priestly sons. Although they were ineffective priests, Eli allowed them to continue in ministry. As punishment, God determined that none of his sons would succeed him, that Eli and his sons would meet an untimely death, that no petition from Samuel to set aside that judgment would be honored. Third, Samuel faced an adoptive father the next morning who wanted to know what God had said to him. Samuel told Eli everything God had told him. To Samuel's surprise, Eli accepted God's judgment graciously. Days before, Eli had already heard the news from a man of God sent his way. Had Samuel misrepresented the truth, his ministry would have been compromised right from the start. Last but not least, Samuel said yes to God whom he knew had high performance expectations. God expected Samuel's leadership to exceed that of Eli.

Every day that we serve as God's representatives, the same expectations facing Samuel will be ours as well. We are expected to perform at a high level. Performing at a high level has nothing to do with being the best DS or DCM so that we might be praised by the church and win awards. God called us to these offices to use us to forward the kingdom on earth as in heaven. Nothing approaching our best selves will evolve unless we use "the means of grace," undergo a circumcision of the heart, and master "the use of money." Furthermore, think about all the laity, pastors, District Superintendents, Directors of Connectional Ministries, and bishops who have come your way. Think more about the spoken and unspoken expectations of yours they never met satisfactorily. Ponder the fact that you are now in their shoes. Those whom you now serve look forward to your leadership with great anticipation. Far more serious, the God of Abraham, Isaac, and Jacob, the God of Sarah, Rachel, and Elizabeth desires far more than they ever will. Do you have a heart for Christ and his church? Let me say it differently.

The day Eli and his sons died, Samuel succeeded Eli. Administering the religious work at Shiloh fell to him. In the struggle to maintain Israel's presence as a nation in the ancient world, Samuel turned military leader, doing battle with the Philistines. More than that, Samuel became a sainted and honored judge in the history of Israel. He anointed Saul and David as the first and second kings of Israel. Two books in the Jewish Canon were named after him. First and Second Samuel can be taken as a major sign of his great contributions to the building of God's kingdom on earth. Last, but certainly not least, Hannah's promise to God was vindicated. She had a son, and God received a great man of God for the people of God.

Some of you might be asking me silently, "Bishop, are we expected to go and do likewise?" Unequivocally yes, remembering this adage shared by the late Supreme Court Justice Thurgood Marshall. Reporters asked Thurgood Marshall what he wanted folk to say about him upon his passing. Marshall responded thus, "Say he did the best he could with what he had!" Samuel's call to ministry was a tough call rooted in his mother's sacrifice, rooted in preparation and God's call in the night, rooted in high performance expectations.

A songwriter gives voice and tune to Samuel's call in the night. May the concluding lines of "Here I Am, Lord" remind you of your call to ministry and renew your commitment to be a servant leader.

> I will go, Lord, if you lead me.
> I will hold your people in my heart.

Amen.

Section Four

ARTICLES

A WINDOW OF OPPORTUNITY

Ernest S. Lyght

L ife is difficult. The storms of life rage periodically and cause sorrow and pain in one's personal life. Some of life's storms are illness, death, unemployment, divorce, doubt, fear, war, poverty, and natural disasters. Such factors as these can be overwhelming at times.

Life also can be difficult for a congregation as it faces changing demographics, a declining membership, increased costs, an aging membership, and an indifferent culture. These dynamics can engender significant fear in a congregation.

How does one respond to the personal crises in life that threaten one's future? How does a congregation respond to crises that jeopardize its very existence? There are no easy answers to these questions. The concept of opportunity, however, comes to mind when I consider these crucial questions.

What is opportunity? Opportunity can be defined as a favorable occasion or circumstance. Consider these synonyms for opportunity: chance, opening, break, and occasion. Opportunity is closely aligned with time. When is the appropriate time? Individuals perhaps are seeking an opportunity to be "successful." Congregations are usually seeking to carry out their mission, which is to "make disciples of Jesus Christ for the transformation of the world."

When the national space agency is planning to launch a rocket into space, the scientists and engineers routinely establish the "window of opportunity," where the weather conditions are acceptable for a launch. In other words, at what time will the rocket be launched, realizing that it needs to be launched at the appropriate and predetermined time, under the right conditions? This time frame is more commonly known as a window of opportunity. The rocket must be launched during the appropriate window of opportunity; otherwise, the launch must be delayed.

Omar Idn Al-Halif once said, "There are four things that come not back: the spoken word, the spent arrow, the past life, and the missed opportunity." The words that we speak should be chosen carefully, because words can hurt and words can heal. Once spoken, words cannot be taken back. The spent arrow is gone forever, and it will do damage wherever it lands. In the same manner, the past is over and gone. As much as we might want to reclaim the past, it cannot be erased, nor can the past be rewritten, because the past is the record of what we do today.

The fourth category is the "missed opportunity," which is a factor in all of life, both individual and corporate. The Easter event (table, cross, and empty tomb) provided and continues to provide an opportunity for God's people to live a life that is sustained by resurrection power. That means that God gives us the opportunity to live a life in Christ Jesus. Some people choose not to seize this opportunity for new life in Jesus Christ. The song, "I've Decided to Make Jesus My Choice," is apropos here: "Some folks would rather have houses and land, . . . I've decided to make Jesus my choice." Choosing appropriate opportunities is at the center of Christian living.

Does not the same principle apply to congregations and congregational life? Congregations are faced with making choices. Will we as a congregation engage in meaningful ministry and missions, or will we simply take care of our building and our own needs? The Healthy Church Assessment process that the West Virginia Conference is engaged in at this time is a process that provides the opportunity for a congregation to assess its own health. The process offers the opportunity for a congregation to determine its own ministry plan for engaging in ministry and missions.

The neglected opportunity does not come back. Think about it!

CARE-FILLED DISCIPLESHIP

Ernest S. Lyght

Recently, while waiting in an airport, I watched a couple providing care for their infant son. The baby did not seem to have a care in the world so long as he was well-fed, warm, dry, and generally comfortable. His parents were very attentive in their care.

As I watched this family, I thought about the care that I received during my adolescent years. My parents provided food, shelter, understanding, discipline, education, and love. Their care for me was immense, and their taking care of me was done without reservation.

Have you ever stopped to think about the meaning of the word *care?* Have you pondered the care that you have received and the care that you have provided to others? The noun *care* is defined as a "feeling of anxiety or concern." We use the expression "not a care in the world." Care also has to do with giving attention or having a watchful regard. Care is dynamic because it is active and can be a positive or negative expression. An example of this is a parent who says to a child, "I really care about your future." The opposite example is a child who says to a parent, "I don't care about going to college."

There are times in life when we feel that nobody cares. Have you ever been in that place? When I am in that place, I am reminded of one of the Beatitudes: "Blessed are the merciful, for they will receive mercy" (Matt 5:7). We want to receive mercy from God and the people around us. This verse, however, is saying that those who are merciful will receive mercy.

Eugene Peterson translates this verse in a helpful way. "You're blessed when you care. At the moment of being 'care-full,' you find yourselves cared for" (Matt 5:7 *The Message*).

EASTER IS LENT'S
ULTIMATE JOY

Ernest S. Lyght

For the pilgrim disciple, Lent is an annual journey, and it provides for us opportunities to tell our faith stories. Ann Weems in her poem "Lent" says that

> Lent is a time to take the time
>   to let the power of our faith story take hold of us.

The Lenten journey, of course, begins with Ash Wednesday and ends with Easter. This year, although Ash Wednesday came early on the calendar, we already had removed all the signs of Christmas.

When Lent begins, we meet the faith questions head-on: Do we know the Jesus whose birth we celebrated at Christmastime? Do we accept this Jesus as our Lord and Savior?

The journey from Ash Wednesday to Easter is a long walk, and we do so reluctantly. It is appropriate, then, that we ask God to grant us courage, forgiveness, and a renewed faith along this walk. A renewed faith will enable us to take up our lives and walk (see Ann Weems, "The Walk"). We do not have to walk alone, because we walk with Jesus, and we walk with one another.

Annually we celebrate the birthday of Martin Luther King, Jr., on January 15, and we memorialize his death on April 4. King was on the path to freedom, but he also was on the journey with Jesus. He knew Jesus, and he affirmed Jesus as his Lord and Savior. Because he walked with Jesus he was able to practice nonviolent resistance and go to prison and suffer abuse from the hands of his opponents/detractors. He believed that God would comfort him even in the presence of his enemies. King sacrificed his life for the sake of the disinherited. Clearly, his faith story intertwined with the faith stories of Jesus that he knew so well.

Martin Luther King devoted himself to three practices that, when employed, can help us on the Lenten journey. He practiced the disciplines of prayer, Bible study, and meditation (communing with God). It is also helpful to remember that King knew the stories of Jesus and he struggled to apply the learning from those stories to his own living. William H. Parker captured the power of the Jesus stories in his hymn, "Tell Me the Stories of Jesus":

> Into the city I'd follow the children's band,
> waving a branch of the palm tree high in my hand;
> one of his heralds, yes, I would sing
> loudest hosannas, "Jesus is King!"

The story of Holy Week is powerful and transforming. Jesus went into Jerusalem on the back of a donkey, and he was treated as a hero by some and disdained by others. In a cogent way, Ann Weems reminds us that "The way to Jerusalem / is cluttered" by life.

The Last Supper and Judas's betrayal, Jesus' death on the cross and Peter's denial, and Jesus' entombment in a borrowed tomb and Jesus' victory over death manifested in his glorious resurrection punctuate the Holy Week story that begins with seeming triumph.

As a local church pastor, I came to understand the transforming power of the Holy Week events in the lives of God's pilgrim disciples in a fresh way. When we celebrate the Lord's Supper on Maundy Thursday, we relive the dynamics of Jesus' last meal with his disciples: acceptance, betrayal, denial, desertion, lagging faith. When we meet Jesus at the cross on Good Friday, we encounter sorrow, pain, forgiveness, and death. On Easter morning, however, we encounter the risen Lord. We see victory in Jesus.

It is useful and important for United Methodists in the West Virginia Conference to tell the stories of Jesus and relive the events of Holy Week each year in our Maundy Thursday services, Good Friday services, and Easter services. Perhaps there are no services more meaningful and transforming in our lives than these.

We are indeed Easter people. The journey through Lent helps us engage Jesus yet again as we seek to be faithful disciples of Jesus. As Easter people, we are empowered to go into the world and make disciples.

HUMOR AND HOLINESS

Ernest S. Lyght

Aunt Marie, my maternal aunt, died on August 9, 2005, at the age of ninety-one years. She was an elementary schoolteacher by profession and taught in the public schools of Maryland for more than forty years. Aunt Marie was a dedicated teacher of excellence and always full of fun and laughter.

A former supervisor and friend shared the following reflections at the time of her death. First, she insisted that all children apply themselves. Second, she would review the assigned material until her students understood their lesson. Third, she believed that all children could learn but not necessarily at the same pace. Finally, her lesson plan always singled out one student every day so that she could make that child feel good about himself or herself.

Always young at heart, Marie never allowed her nephews and nieces to address her as Aunt Marie; it was simply Marie. Although Marie did not have any children of her own, she loved children dearly.

Marie had a great sense of humor and loved to tell stories about her students. It was fun to hear her stories because they were so humorous, and she would laugh so heartily while telling her stories. She would literally take on the character of the people in the story.

Oh yes, she loved to tell stories about us (my two sisters, my brother, and me). Marie visited our home often and observed the funny things that we said and did during our adolescent years. She did not hesitate to reenact these events at family gatherings.

Marie said that as a very young boy, I chastised my father's sister one morning while she was fixing breakfast for the family. Aunt Phoene was preparing eggs and inadvertently discarded a few whole eggs into the garbage along with the empty eggshells. I reputedly said to Aunt Phoene, "Why are you wasting my mother's eggs? Are you *crazy?*" (Imagine that.) Marie, of course, had to rescue me from my errant response and save me from the wrath of Aunt Phoene and my parents. Wow, that was a narrow escape for a little kid!

I have fond memories of the wonderful telephone conversations that I had with Marie, especially in recent years. Some days I would call her and the conversation would begin with Marie indicating that she was "doing fairly well." As the conversation unfolded, invariably we would begin to talk about things spiritual, and we would reminisce about some comical events that we had shared together. The conversation would be flavored with a mixture of humor and holiness. Those were sacred moments.

One day Marie was in the lunchroom at her elementary school and she heard loud noises coming from one of the tables where several students were seated. She noticed that a young student was beating the table alternately with his fork, knife, and spoon. He was getting very noisy indeed. Marie asked him what he was doing, and he let her know that he was offering a blessing over the food before his classmates ate their lunch. He said, "The Bible says praise the Lord."

Marie gently corrected him and shared the relevant Scripture passage with him: "Let everything that breathes praise the LORD!" (Ps 150:6). She reminded the youngster that forks, knives, and spoons do not have breath. But we who have breath can use such objects to praise God. The objects themselves cannot praise God.

Marie praised the Lord as long as she had breath. She also continued to laugh even when she was not feeling well. It was the blending of humor and holiness that coursed its way through Marie's life journey.

Surely God invites each one of us to possess a sense of humor. God also invites us to experience a sense of holiness in life, for all of life is sacred, even that which is humorous.

ORDER OUR STEPS

Ernest S. Lyght

In this season of Thanksgiving–Advent–Christmas–New Year, I am reminded of one of my favorite contemporary gospel songs, "Order My Steps." The lyrics express a prayer request to God: "Order my steps in Your word, dear Lord."

As we make our way through the Advent season on the journey to Christmas, I am compelled to pause and wonder about our steps in a world that is ever changing. We are a nation at war, and we are living in fear of terrorism. We are a nation divided and stamped with labels, such as liberal or conservative, Democrat or Republican, rich or poor, and proabortion or antiabortion. Does God care about all of this? No, God does not care about these labels, because Jesus is neither a democrat nor a republican.

God, however, does care about our spiritual life: "For God so loved the world that he gave his only Son, so that everyone who believes in him may not perish but may have eternal life" (John 3:16). The gospel writer, John, notes that the Word in the beginning of time was with God and the Word was God. This "Word became flesh and lived among us, and we have seen his glory, the glory as of a father's only son, full of grace and truth" (John 1:14).

Although the world is ever changing, our God remains the same and is ready to order our steps when we ask God to teach us God's will. But there is so much that gets in our way and blocks the path that we would walk with Jesus.

Christmas is coming, so we proclaim "joy to the world," because Jesus is coming. We, therefore, want to prepare room for Jesus. We want to clear a place for Jesus in our hearts. There is a television program called *Clean Sweep*, and it is about families that want or need to make room in their homes so that their home life will become less cluttered. In other words, they want or need to get rid of all the junk around them, but they usually cannot decide what to get rid of, so they take no action to remove the clutter.

We sometimes experience such a clutter in our spiritual life, and we fail to take the needed action to remove the clutter. A key to transforming a cluttered life into a more orderly life is to prepare room for Jesus, the Word, full of grace and truth. The gospel song "Order My Steps" suggests an approach to this transformation.

> Order my steps in Your word.
> Order my tongue in Your word.

This way of living would require us to change our path and eliminate some of the places that we have visited in the past. It would require us to speak in a different manner with a new vocabulary. It would require God to bathe our hearts with God's love so that we might love with compassion and understanding. It would require us to open the door to our hearts.

Here are a few questions to ponder. Is there sufficient room in your heart for Jesus? Have you allocated sufficient time in your life for daily personal devotions (prayer, Bible study, and reflection)? Is there time in your schedule for participation in a group Bible study and regular attendance at public worship services? When we answer yes to these questions, then we are demonstrating our willingness to immerse our whole being in God's written word and the living Word, Jesus Christ.

In this holy season, let us prepare new room for Jesus Christ in our hearts and allow God to order our steps in God's living Word.

SOMETHING NEW WITH GOD

Ernest S. Lyght

When it comes to New Year's resolutions, the truth of the matter is that I do not compile a list of New Year's resolutions at the end of the year. I do not believe in such resolutions. For all practical purposes these resolutions are just about useless. They may make me feel good at the time, but I tend to forget them in a few weeks. So I don't make New Year's resolutions. Do you?

A New Year's resolution often suggests that one is going to stop doing something or start doing something. I am going to stop smoking. I am going to lose weight. I am going to be more loving and caring. I will not drink alcoholic beverages anymore. I will be more faithful in my church worship attendance. I am going to become a tither. Do such resolutions, and others like them, have any depth of meaning for the one who makes the resolution?

Where is God in my resolution? Where is God in my life? Where is God in the life of my worshiping congregation? If my resolution is rooted in my will, then that resolution likely fails. On the other hand, a resolution that is rooted in God's will, as discerned in conversation with God, will be accomplished in God's time.

Mary and Joseph wanted to get married and live a normal life like ordinary people. God, however, intervened in their lives, and Mary became the mother of Jesus. That was God's will, not Mary's will. Mary's relative, Elizabeth, also was subject to God's will. Elizabeth, although elderly, conceived a son. The birth of Elizabeth's son was God's will. The birth was not the will of Elizabeth. In these two historic events, we see that "nothing will be impossible with God" (Luke 1:37). What is required is that we listen to God. In our listening we come to believe, obey, and serve. Mary and Elizabeth listened to God. Mary and Elizabeth obeyed God. Mary and Elizabeth served God.

Are we willing to listen to God at year's end in an effort to discern God's will for our lives? What is God's yearning for you as a pilgrim disciple? What is God's yearning for the congregation of which you are a member? What is God's yearning for the West Virginia Conference? There are no easy answers to these questions. Yet we must ponder these queries as we seek to be faithful disciples of Jesus Christ. Is God trying to do something new?

Jesus came into the world and lived among us. He brought a bundle of new ideas that disrupted the lives of individuals who listened to him. Lives are disrupted because accepting the ideas and teachings of Jesus will bring about a deep change in one's way of knowing, believing, being, and doing. One will be a new creation. Now that is an awesome gift from God.

We face the new year with a multitude of memories from the year just ended. We have fond memories and memories of events and experiences that we would rather blot out. Will the new year bring peace, healing, and wholeness in one's life? Will we resolve our personal "resolutions" (problems, issues, concerns, conflicts, desires)? I am reminded of the words of the hymn, "It is no secret what God can do."

The good news is that all things are possible with God. Something new with God requires openness on our part. Open your mind to the kingdom-living ideas of Jesus. Open your heart to the warmth of God's radical love. Open the door of your life to God's will that alters one's life in new and fresh ways. Such openness on the part of the pilgrim disciple and the worshiping congregation leads to the experience of God doing something new.

Like Mary, let us ponder this in our hearts.

THE JOURNEY: FROM ASHES TO RESURRECTION

Ernest S. Lyght

There are two basic questions that many people ask multiple times during the course of a day. What time is it? Where am I? We can determine the time by looking at our watch or a nearby clock. We can determine our location by looking at our surroundings and reading the street signs or road signs. When we are driving on the highway, there might not be a nearby sign of any kind. Modern technology, however, has resolved this dilemma.

Many automobiles are equipped with a Global Positioning System (GPS). The GPS is a satellite-based navigation system made up of a network of satellites. The GPS works in any weather conditions, anywhere in the world, twenty-four hours a day. Yes, the system is free to its users.

GPS receivers take information transmitted from the satellites and use triangulation to calculate the user's exact location. This is useful information when you need to know your location and how to get to your desired location. The GPS can guide a traveler from one place to another place as desired by the traveler.

As we prepare to embark on the Lenten journey, from Ash Wednesday to Easter Sunday, we should ponder this spiritual question: Where am I in relationship to God? Do you know where you are spiritually? Do you know where you need to be spiritually? Peter denied Jesus and watched from a distance as Jesus was taken to the cross and crucified. Judas left Jesus and turned his back on Jesus as he betrayed him. The other ten disciples left Jesus and took flight, separating themselves from their spiritual leader. None of these biblical characters understood that they needed to know their faith position at this point on their journey with Jesus.

Perhaps these followers of Jesus did not realize that it is helpful to know your faith position in relationship to Jesus? They did not have a

GPS receiver available to tell them just how far they had drifted from the heart of Jesus. Neither did the three kings have a GPS receiver to lead them to Jesus' birthplace. They followed a distant star. When they returned home, they traveled back by a different route and apparently did not get lost.

Our participation in the life, suffering, death, resurrection, and ascension of Jesus Christ is at the heart of the Christian faith. We declare that "the Word became flesh and lived among us" (John 1:14). In Jesus, God was reconciling humankind to God's heart. In the season of Lent and Easter, we remember and honor the mystery of our redemption. It is hoped that Jesus' death and resurrection will help shape us as Spirit-filled disciples of Jesus Christ. Ash Wednesday marks a time for fresh beginnings in the faith, a time for returning to God. During Lent, we strive to set aside our sins in anticipation of becoming recipients of God's amazing grace.

One approach to Lent and the opportunity for penance is to engage in prayer and some form of fasting. Scripture, however, cautions us about our prayer posture and our rationale for fasting. First, with regard to prayer, we should avoid any public display. The better approach is this: "But whenever you pray, go into your room and shut the door and pray to your Father who is in secret; and your Father who sees in secret will reward you" (Matt 6:6).

Second, in relationship to fasting, consider this approach: "But when you fast, put oil on your head and wash your face, so that your fasting may be seen not by others but by your Father who is in secret; and your Father who sees in secret will reward you" (Matt 6:17-18). Prayer and fasting are the engines that drive the pilgrim disciple on the Lenten journey from Ash Wednesday to Easter.

Do you know where you are on your spiritual journey? Are you seeking to come closer to God through Jesus Christ? Just turn on your GPS system: God, Prayer, and Sacrifice. First, acknowledge God as our creator and sustainer. Second, be in conversation with God through daily prayer. Third, when fasting, be sure to make a sacrifice that removes that which is separating you from God and keeps you telling your own story rather than God's story. Now measure the result of this triangulation.

The poem of Cleland B. McAfee provides insight for us on this Lenten journey:

There is a place of quiet rest,
near to the heart of God;
a place where sin cannot molest,
near to the heart of God.

The refrain says:

O Jesus, blest Redeemer,
sent from the heart of God,
hold us who wait before thee
near to the heart of God.

When we come near to the heart of God, we encounter joy and peace.

We need Jesus to lead us near to the heart of God. That is the aim of the Lenten journey. Let us ponder this in our hearts as we prepare for the journey from Ash Wednesday to Easter.

NO ANSWERS, JUST QUESTIONS

Jonathan D. Keaton

One of my daughters summoned me to step on a large black ant in my home office. I refused. My refusal sparked an ethical dialogue. Ordinarily I'd put the ant outside, but it was past midnight. So, I offered to get rid of him using bug spray. She protested. "Spraying would cause an elongated painful death," she countered. If I stepped on him, "death would be immediate and therefore no suffering." Undaunted, I offered to toss him in the toilet. She protested even more. "Drowning the ant would be worse than bug spray," she said. Then I countered, "If you want him dead, you're going to have to step on him yourself." With that, I left the room. All the while, the ant didn't move, as if listening to our conversation. Later that day, I told my wife about it. My wife already knew. Our daughter beat me to the punch. "What happened to the ant?" I asked. My wife replied, "Our daughter didn't step on him, either." An ethical dialogue over how the ant should be executed resulted in his life being spared.

Another member of the animal kingdom was not so fortunate! The same daughter and I were in the kitchen when we heard a loud thump. Something hit the house. So, I rushed to investigate. On the outside porch, a large robin lay flat on his back, critically injured. I notified my daughter, who is supersensitive to the animal world. The robin needed first aid; we had to provide it. But when I returned, it was too late. Apparently, the robin had mistakenly flown straight into the house going full bore. His death shocked and silenced us momentarily. In an attempt to revive him, I offered to pour a plastic tumbler of water over him. My daughter objected, saying, "He might drown." She accepted my alternate plan to sprinkle him. Sprinkling had no effect. The bird's tragic death evoked compassion. But this dad had no words to comfort a daughter empathetic to the animal kingdom with the exception of spiders, certain insects, and large ants invading her space.

Surprise and shock greeted me on Interstate 96 East. No sooner had I entered I-96 at Okemos Road than a motorcyclist sped by going well past the speed limit. Suddenly, he let out a loud yell, kicked his bike up on one wheel, and raced down the interstate. He left me and other cars in the dust. My mouth flew open in horror. Time stood still as I watched the helmeted, black jacket–wearing motorcyclist hover between life, death, and serious injury, speeding along on one wheel. Back down on two wheels, the motorcyclist disappeared in the traffic heading toward Detroit. By God's grace, he survived to ride another day. I saw it; but I still can't believe it.

Stories have transforming power. Of late, I have been thinking on these things. You know how it is—*no answers, just questions.*

SHOULD WE OR SHOULDN'T WE?

Jonathan D. Keaton

Conferences like Greater New Jersey, Great Rivers (Illinois), Missouri, and Arkansas have addressed the should-we-or-should-we-not-merge question with a yes. They believed that mission and ministry could be done more efficiently and effectively that way. Other conferences have said no. United Methodists in Michigan turned away from merger in 1995. Yet the question has reappeared. When the Detroit and West Michigan Annual Conferences passed the resolution below, the consideration of merger or creating something new was inevitable. The 2004 legislation read: "Be it resolved that Bishop Linda Lee appoint a task force to explore *all* ways that Detroit Annual Conference and the West Michigan Annual Conference can cooperate in ministry, both to be more effective in ministry and to be good stewards of financial resources."

Exploring *all* ways both conferences might cooperate led us down two paths: (1) to ask equivalent boards, agencies, and constituencies to meet and investigate ways to cooperate to avoid duplication and reduce costs and so on and (2) to propose that West Michigan and Detroit Annual Conferences become one. With respect to comparable entities, we have seen fruit already. For instance, both Councils on Finance and Administration (CFA) have shared fiscal and interpretive information. CFA and the Board of Pensions have gotten excited about the possibility of cutting health insurance costs if an insurer provided quality coverage at a lower cost. Our Conference Council on Ministries Staffs has conferred about camping ministries, youth and young adults, and a host of other ministries that would be enhanced by cooperation. With respect to creating something new, that has occurred. Subject to the will of both annual conferences, the United Methodist Foundations of each conference will become one. After protracted discussion and research, they have concluded it is possible to serve the church better, together.

Is the bishop guaranteeing that merger will make us more efficient and effective and lower costs? No, I am not. Nothing is automatic. Personnel, policy and policy matters, loss of identity and leadership positions, and appointment issues demand careful attention. However, mergers in the conferences mentioned above prove that partnering together does work, that something new and better can emerge. Perhaps we need to see the question of creating something new as a gift. As a new baby offers great possibility for two parents, so does one conference. So choose. In your choosing, let this bishop make one thing perfectly clear. *I am still persuaded that our major task is making disciples for Jesus Christ. Holding before the church yearly growth goals of 10 percent in membership and 5 percent in apportionment giving is my vision.* Nothing we are going to do, want to do, or want to try and no complaint, theological squabble, or new creation will lead this bishop away from laying the burden of disciple-making upon every church, lay-, and clergyperson within the sound of my voice or the reach of my pen. Whatever structural future we choose, making disciples for Jesus Christ is *my* nonnegotiable. Should we or shouldn't we is never the question.

OUR CONVERTS ARE FEW

Jonathan D. Keaton

Dare I sound the focus of my episcopacy to begin the new year? Unequivocally, yes. Making disciples of Jesus Christ for the transformation of the world will not leave me alone. You, gentle readers, must be weary of this spotlight. This I know: Christ's joyful challenge of disciple-making causes my heart to ache. What pains me all too often is a familiar realization in numerous Methodist circles: *our converts are few*. Surely, I am not bereft of the skills, commitment, or vision of Mr. Wesley, John the Baptist, and Lydia, who started a house church in Acts 16. Or am I?

Upon my 1996 arrival in the East Ohio Conference as bishop-elect, Bishop Boulton passed on to me a book entitled *Sacerdos Et Pontifex*. Bishop Kelley, a Roman Catholic bishop, published it in 1940. A lengthy quote from the author has torn at my spirit ever since. His words have served as a disturbing mirror with regard to my own disciple-making. Bishop Kelley wrote, "It is your own soul that comes first. Only when that is safe will the overflow of good from it help others. You can do all things, but only in Him that sent you." Kelley went on to say,

> That lesson I did not learn early enough, or rather did not fully understand from the beginning; not indeed until the fever of action had long had a grip on me. Consequently I feel that for me there were many lost years. I did go out on the highways and by the hedges and I was an ardent and zealous servant. I organized, I wrote, I went to conventions. Did I get anything more out of it all than a transient reputation? Almost nothing. There arose a disturbing fact to face me: *my converts were few*. I know other priests who apparently had not been one-tenth as zealous as myself, priests who could not be dragged to conventions, who scarcely ever left the confines of their parishes, *but who had the spiritual children denied me*. . . . You may be inclined—and in perfect

good faith—to say that I am exaggerating, that indirectly I must have made hosts of converts. *But if I did, I was denied the joy of meeting and instructing them.*

Far too often, this has been my fate. Still, I press on toward the mark described in Matthew 28:19-20. Pray for me.

BOMBS BURSTING IN AIR

Jonathan D. Keaton

Come, Lord Jesus. Prince of Peace, be born in us today. Your people tire of "bombs bursting in air." In the subways of London, the streets of Paris, the hotels of Amman, Jordan, on the battlefields of Iraq, Iran, and Afghanistan. "Bombs burst in air," killing those you came to save. Your people called Methodists tire of "bombs bursting in air" unleashed by Judicial Council rulings. Opining about ordination, pastoral discretion, homosexuality, domestic partner benefits, and related issues of religion and race, all sides drop verbal shrapnel on the other, maiming those whom you came to save. Come, Holy Child of Bethlehem. The streets of your hometown are half-empty. Rachel's tomb is closed. Violent clashes between Palestinians and Israelis are to blame. Although folks come and go in relative safety, there is no peace. Any act of provocation or misunderstanding can turn Bethlehem into a war zone instantaneously, eliminating those whom you came to save. Forgive us. Save us, Emmanuel. You who hath clean hands and a pure heart. Lord, may we so care for your safety and presence that our swords become ploughshares, our spears become pruning hooks, and our mouths spew forth the love of John 3:16. Come, eschatological promise cited in the third stanza of a beloved Christmas carol. John T. McFarland, a Methodist minister, adds this verse to "Away in a Manger" in the early 1900s:

> Be near me, Lord Jesus, I ask thee to stay
> close by me forever, and love me, I pray;
> bless *all* the dear children in thy tender care,
> and fit us for heaven, to live with thee there.

Fit us for living now, Lord, even as "the bombs are bursting in air."

HURRICANE KATRINA

Jonathan D. Keaton

NOW that we've heard about *old* reports from the Army Corps of Engineers concluding that levees surrounding New Orleans could barely withstand a category 3 hurricane, unlike category-4 Katrina, but politics stymied complete restoration and improvements;

NOW that we've learned how insensitive FEMA and other U.S. officials were, who waited up to seventy-two hours to address one of America's greatest natural disasters before scalding criticism shook them from their lethargy;

NOW that we've *scolded* the poor and the destitute for not leaving low-lying areas along the Gulf Coast of Alabama, Mississippi, and Louisiana when they had no mode of transportation and the first law of nature was in full swing;

NOW that we've labeled American citizens victimized by Katrina as looters, evacuees, refugees, hoi polloi, poor folk, mentally deficient, and other negative stereotypes;

NOW that we've heard horror stories of the Superdome becoming a super field of *dread* with depression, disease, despair, and death as its star players;

NOW that the dead floating in contaminated water have suddenly become objects of media respect a fortnight after Katrina's advent;

NOW that the deadly force of Hurricane Katrina once more exposed the myth that America is the world's *only* superpower (that title belongs to God alone), let the compassionate spirit of the good Samaritan in every American supersede armchair critiques and finger-pointing so that levees are rebuilt, the cities drained, the land cleared, the homeless sheltered, the hungry fed, the naked clothed, the stranger welcomed, the sick healed, the separated united, and the dead buried.

May it be so as we pray daily, give much, and do all we can to assist survivors of Katrina entering our communities across the nation!

Section Five

PRAYERS, MEDITATIONS, AND MEANDERINGS

IN SUFFERING, HOPE: A MEDITATION

Edsel A. Ammons

Read Isaiah 55:1-9

*Why do you spend your money for that which is not bread,
and your labor for that which does not satisfy?*

There are times when we are tempted to say, like Job,

> Affliction does not come from the dust,
> Neither does trouble sprout from the ground,
> For [men and women are] born for trouble. (5:6 NASB)

But thanks to the one whose trial and triumph are like our own and who bears the name of the mighty prophet Isaiah, we know better and cannot be satisfied with such an answer to the pain that grips our hearts. Faith will not let us fold our hands and give in to suffering or admit that suffering is the common lot of us all, but through God's divine grace, we can turn the worst tragedy into the stuff of a new life of high aspirations.

The voice of hope in this Scripture passage was that of a great soul. We know this, though we do not know his name. Scholars agree that he is not the same man who spoke with authority in the first half of the great book of Isaiah. Perhaps he was too busy at this work to leave his autograph. Perhaps it was because the intent of his message was to comfort his exiled people, to assure them that God would put down the oppressor, Babylon, and set them free. Yes, it does happen that way when the storms of life are raging. And none of us is spared. Faith does not shield or make winners of us in the game of life (despite the claims of athletes and some preachers). Faith does properly instruct us that when life knocks us off our feet, we are held up by something or Someone who is more than the sum of all our suffering. Nor can we find refuge in some new philosophy or impressive argument. That may be difficult to accept, for we are the children of the Enlightenment, who believe that the way out of every dilemma is found in neatly wrapped logic or reason. Not so with this prophet. Facing up to the miseries confronting him and his people, he turned to God. That enabled him to withstand the stones that were falling upon their lives and to turn them into stepping-stones to great spiritual strength.

Speaking to the distressed of his day, those leading starved lives bereft of satisfaction, the prophet asks, "Why do you spend your money for that which is not bread, / and your labor for that which does not satisfy?" Notice the tone of the prophet's question, which is not a condemnation. Some among them are wastrels no doubt, but others also are decent and faithful. Faith like the prophet's speaks to all. He speaks to those who worship the wrong god—like an old habit, stifling tradition, or undeserved wealth whose mad-seeking promises only wreck themselves and injure others. The diligent seeking of some leads to things that are wise and are enriching to life. All are seekers, but only a few are finders. Nor do we speak ill of either, aware that our own selfish ways lead to our starvation.

What does the prophet say to us who often seek for what cannot satisfy? Only that our failure is because we look in the wrong direction, that the greatest sadness results from the decision to be satisfied with what we are. Such satisfaction with himself and the prodigal would never have risen about the hogs and the husks. The cure for our soul sickness comes by finding God. He urges, "Everyone who thirsts, / come to the waters" and drink what alone can quench your thirst (v. 1). The bread you are buying has no nutritional value. You need the water and the bread of life. Like the One who would come centuries later, he speaks of fullness of life that is of God alone. "Seek the LORD while he may be found, / call upon him while he is near" (v. 6). Forsake your unrighteous, sinful ways. Find joy in a new relationship with God. We were created to live in such relationship. Hope and the salvation born of such hope will come in no other way and will make us new creations.

A lay poet tells of how one day as she was washing dishes, a small dark-colored bug suddenly appeared from she knew not where and slowly moved across the sink toward her. An ordinary-looking bug—no bright colors, no odd-shaped body, no outstanding features of any kind. On closer examination, she saw that it had wings and could fly! She was strangely moved. At times like the one we are living through, we become aware of how ordinary we are, feel frustrated when pain and distress over-take us. Remember with the prophet that God has given us wings to fly—spiritual wings of faith and hope that lift us over our frustration and our suffering.

Prayer: Eternal and almighty God, inspire us to find our way ever closer to you so that in every moment and circumstance of life we shall cling to the faith that enables us to persevere in the hope that sustains and empowers us. In Jesus' name, amen.

A Prayer for Peace

Edsel A. Ammons

God of tender mercies,
In the midst of troublesome days and anxious nights, we thank you that our restless hearts continue to seek after you in whom they will find rest. Thank you for the inspiration of your spirit, which makes us as concerned for our neighbor's well-being as we are for our own. And thank you for your word of comfort and the perspective it brings to tragedy and disappointment.

Forgive us for yielding to the temptation of pride and self-sufficiency, for daring to believe that some of us are more deserving than others of your grace and mercy, for failure to know that your love makes no such distinction and embraces all of your children with no exception.

Forgive our easy confusion of power with the presumption of privilege, our abundance with entitlement, or strength of nation with bestowal of divine favor. Forgive our sin and transform mind and heart for the sake of the righteousness, which is your special promise and gift to all of your creation.

Even as we anticipate the end of another tragic war and the safe return of most of our sons and daughters, our celebrations are sobered by thoughts of our wounded and dead. Nor do we treat lightly or with indifference the pain and horror experienced by those we call enemy.

Teach us, O Lord, that differences of religion or politics or national origin, though factors of significance in the unfolding human discourse, are also subservient to your ultimate will for this good earth and its people.

Come, O loving God, and speak your clear word of life and hope. Grant us renewed devotion to the Lord of peace, who alone can give us the peace and comfort for which we yearn. Put in our hearts the prophet's scorn of tyranny and an unyielding resolve to worship you rather than the powers of evil, to entrust our future to "Gideon's few" rather than to Caesar's multitudes. Free us from hardness of heart and wanderings of mind and spirit, which are the breeding places of hatred, and the impulse to violence and war so that we learn how to overcome evil with good and how to beat our swords into pruning forks.

Merciful God, you did not wait for us to deserve the sacrifice of your Son; you do not wait even yet for us to deserve your offer of eternal life. In contrition, we pray again: Do not wait until we deserve peace; grant peace in our time. We pray in the name of Jesus Christ our Lord. Amen.

Prayer at the End of the Day

Edsel A. Ammons

O God, in whose presence our souls take delight, on whom in affliction we call; our comfort by day, our song in the night, our hope, our salvation, our all. We come to the close of another day grateful for your abiding presence and for our continued awareness that no matter the nature of our thought, word, or deed, we remain close to you—as close as the air we breathe.

Our faith is made strong, Eternal God, as we have acknowledged the truth given to the saints of old and to us that the day now closing has been a day "which the Lord has made; thus, we have rejoiced and been glad in it." Enable us in these moments of prayerful reflections to remember everyone—family and friends and those whose names are not known to us—with the hope that they will feel the power of your spirit as the day and the night unfold in ways unique to them and to all who are of their households.

Master of the troubled waters of life, give to us quiet rest through this night and heartfelt peace in blessed sleep and in our anticipation of the dawn of a new day. We entrust our well-being into your powerful hands. Strong deliverer, be thou still our strength and shield. And now, merciful Savior, receive this prayer in the spirit in which it is offered and I shall give you thanks in the name of Jesus Christ, our Lord, amen.

A Eulogy: In Memory of Clarice Townsend

Edsel A. Ammons

This is a moment when a death moves us to search for language that rises above expressions that are ordinary and mundane. That was how I felt when son, John Townsend, called to say that his mother had died— Clarice Townsend, matriarch of a remarkable family, dead. I confess to you that it took a while for me to get beyond the initial shock of the call and the word of the loss. In John's voice, however, was a note of both grief and rejoicing as he shared the story of a woman who had been a devoted wife and mother, a woman of the church, a disciple of the Christ of the church, who had endured disease and suffering and triumphed over both. What John conveyed as we talked was his own confident awareness that, even in death, the spirit of Clarice Townsend had prevailed!

She had lived with the scourge and the dread of cancer for a number of years; it was not secret to her or the family or others who knew her. Nor did it prevent the investment of herself in the many ways that she served the church—as an active member of her congregation, which she joined forty-three years ago, in district and annual conference work, especially with United Methodist Women. She was a person of many remarkable gifts and talents—sometimes barely known to those closest to her until, surprisingly, they were given expression in rare and unexpected moments. John described one such moment while visiting his mother not too many months ago. He said he had known of his mother's musical interests and skills, but he was not prepared for what happened when she sat down to the piano and started to play—not chopsticks or a church hymn, but a demanding classical score that he had never heard her even attempt to play before that moment. Yes, she was wonderfully gifted herself, and she did not fail to pass on to her children that same appreciation for music and the arts.

Perhaps you know now why one of the Scripture passages selected for today is from the book of Proverbs, from chapter 31, in particular: A good wife, mother, woman

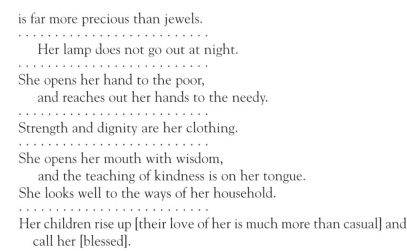

> is far more precious than jewels.
> . . . .
>   Her lamp does not go out at night.
> . . . .
> She opens her hand to the poor,
>   and reaches out her hands to the needy.
> . . . .
> Strength and dignity are her clothing.
> . . . .
> She opens her mouth with wisdom,
>   and the teaching of kindness is on her tongue.
> She looks well to the ways of her household.
> . . . .
> Her children rise up [their love of her is much more than casual] and
>   call her [blessed].
> . . . .
> "Many women have done excellently, but [she surpasses] them all."

Remember, these sentiments are from a Hebrew scribe at a time when such status was not always accorded to women. But whoever offers consolation and comfort, he speaks what our hearts and spirits yearn to hear, "Lo, I am with you always." You will experience heartache and sorrow and death. But be of good cheer; I shall walk that mournful trail with you and will be with you always to the very end. The journey often becomes heavy and burdensome, but take comfort, you'll never be alone in it and in the very midst of it, you will feel the power of God's spirit lifting your own spirit beyond the limitations and the hurt and the heartbreak. That was your mother's witness, John, as she made her way through the death of a spouse of many years, your father, and her own years of failing health and impending death. It helps us understand her great fondness for the familiar Harold Arlen classic, "Somewhere Over the Rainbow."

Happy little bluebirds present no competition to your victorious spirit, Clarice; you are in flight to a land that we have heard of, not in a lullaby but in the gospel; a place not made with hands, where you will rejoice always with the King of kings. Amen.

Notes

Page
4   "I don't know who," from Dag Hammarskjöld, *Markings* (New York: Alfred A. Knopf, 1964), 205.

6   "The real world," from Thomas Merton, "The Cell," from Monica Furlong, *Merton, A Biography* (San Francisco: HarperSanFrancisco, 1980), 80.

6   "One of the most," from ibid.

7   "I cried all night long," from Clara Ward, "Until I Found the Lord," in *Songs of Zion* (Nashville: Abingdon Press, 1981), 177.

37   "Prayer is then," from Diana Butler Bass, "Silent Treatment," *Christian Century* (Sept. 19, 2006): 27.

39   "Why is the faithful," from S T Kimbrough Jr., "Still Shaping Our Faith," *Circuit Rider* (Sept./Oct. 2006): 14.

39   "Only [one] who is," from John Philip Wogaman and Douglas M. Strong, *Readings in Christian Ethics: A Historical Sourcebook* (Louisville: Westminster John Knox, 1996), viii.

44   The five dynamics are from Peter F. Drucker, *The Effective Executive* (New York: Harper & Row, 1966), 166-74.

51   The General Rules, *The Book of Discipline of The United Methodist Church—2004* (Nashville: The United Methodist Publishing House, 2004), 71-74.

51   "The Means of Grace," from "Sermon 16" in *The Sermons of John Wesley, 1872 Edition* (ed. Thomas Jackson; London: Wesleyan Conference Office).

52   "Giving Up for Lent," from Ann Weems, *Putting the Amazing Back in Grace* (Louisville: Westminster John Knox, 1999), 39-51.

53   "Take Time to Be Holy," *The United Methodist Hymnal* (Nashville: The United Methodist Publishing House, 1989), 395.

64   "In spite," from Francis Clement Kelley, *Sacerdos Et Pontifex* (Paterson, N.J.: St. Anthony Guild Press, 1940), 238.

70   "The vocation," from Henri Nouwen, *Reaching Out* (New York: Doubleday, 1975), 46.

73   "What we need," from Robert F. Kennedy, "On the Death of Martin Luther King," http://www.historyplace.com/speeches/rfk.htm. Accessed November 16, 2007.

73   "That will not shrink," from "Prayer for Strong Faith," *Hymns for Christian Devotion* (ed. J. G. Adams and E. H. Chapin; Boston: Abel Tompkins, 1853), 377.

73   The idea that only love can eliminate hate is from Martin Luther King, Jr., "Strength to Love."

74   The challenge to find hope in despair is from Martin Luther King, Jr., "I Have a Dream."

74 The ideal of love and community is from Martin Luther King, Jr., "Letter from Birmingham Jail."

75 "Jesus, Jesus, Jesus!" *The United Methodist Hymnal* (Nashville: The United Methodist Publishing House, 1989), 171.

83 "I am thine," Fanny J. Crosby, *The United Methodist Hymnal* (Nashville: The United Methodist Publishing House, 1989), 419.

84 "There is no," from *The Abingdon Bible Commentary* (ed. Frederick Carl Eiselen, Edwin Lewis, and David G. Downey; Nashville: Abingdon Press, 1929), 385.

85 The ideas for our best selves are from *John Wesley's Forty-Four Sermons* (London: Epworth Press, n.d.), numbers 12, 13, and 44.

86 "Here I Am, Lord," *The United Methodist Hymnal* (Nashville: The United Methodist Publishing House, 1989), 593.

89 "A Window of Opportunity" originally appeared in *The West Virginia United Methodist*, May 2006.

90 "I've Decided to Make Jesus My Choice," Stanley J. Lewis, Su-Ma Publishing Company, A Division of MCS Music America, 1973.

91 "*Care*-filled Discipleship" originally appeared in *The West Virginia United Methodist*, February 2005.

93 'Easter Is Lent's Ultimate Joy" originally appeared in *The West Virginia United Methodist*, March 2005.

93 "Lent Is a Time," from Ann Weems, *Kneeling in Jerusalem* (Louisville: Westminster/John Knox, 1993), 22.

93 "The Walk," from ibid., 21.

94 "Into the city," William H. Parker, *The United Methodist Hymnal* (Nashville: The United Methodist Publishing House, 1989), 277.

94 "The Way to Jerusalem," from Weems, *Kneeling in Jerusalem*, 46.

95 "Humor and Holiness" originally appeared in *The West Virginia United Methodist*, September 2005.

97 "Order Our Steps" originally appeared in *The West Virginia United Methodist*, December 2004.

97 "Order My Steps," Glen Bruleigh, *Order My Steps*, Intersound Records, 1995.

99 "Something New with God" originally appeared in *The West Virginia United Methodist*, January 2007.

100 "It Is No Secret (What God Can Do)," Stuart Hamblen, MCA Records, 1950.

101 "The Journey: From Ashes to Resurrection" originally appeared in *The West Virginia United Methodist*, February 2007.

103 "There Is a Place," *The United Methodist Hymnal* (Nashville: The United Methodist Publishing House, 1989), 472.

105 "No Answers, Just Questions" originally appeared in *The Michigan Christian Advocate*, August 2006.

107 "Should We or Shouldn't We?" originally appeared in *The Michigan Christian Advocate*, April 2006.

109 "Our Converts Are Few" originally appeared in *The Michigan Christian Advocate*, December 2005.

109 "It is your own," from Kelley, *Sacerdos Et Pontifex*.

111 "Bombs Bursting in Air" originally appeared in *The Michigan Christian Advocate*, December 2005.

111 "Away in a Manger," *The United Methodist Hymnal* (Nashville: The United Methodist Publishing House, 1989), 217, emphasis added.

113 "Hurricane Katrina" originally appeared in *The Michigan Christian Advocate*, October 2005.

123 "O God, in whose presence" is based on "O Thou, in Whose Presence," *The United Methodist Hymnal* (Nashville: The United Methodist Publishing House, 1989), 518.